Ms. Cahill
for
Congress

Ms. Cahill

for

Congress

One Fearless Teacher, Her Sixth-Grade Class,
and the Election That Changed Their Lives Forever

Tierney Cahill
and Linden Gross

BALLANTINE BOOKS NEW YORK

A Ballantine Books Trade Paperback Original

Published in the United States by Ballantine Books, an imprint of The Random House Publishing Group, a division of Random House, Inc., New York.

BALLANTINE and colophon are registered trademarks of Random House, Inc.

Library of Congress Cataloging-in-Publication Data
Cahill, Tierney.
Ms. Cahill for Congress : one fearless teacher, her sixth-grade class, and the election that changed their lives forever /
Tierney Cahill and Linden Gross.
p.   cm.
Includes bibliographical references and index.
ISBN 978-0-345-50577-4 (pbk. : alk. paper)
1. Cahill, Tierney. 2. Political candidates—Nevada—Biography.
3. Women political candidates—Nevada—Biography. 4. United States.
Congress. House—Elections, 2000. 5. Political campaigns—Nevada.
6. Nevada—Politics and government. 7. Teachers—Nevada—Biography.
8. Political candidates—United States—Biography. 9. Political
participation—United States—Case studies. I. Gross, Linden. II. Title.
F845.25.C34A3 2008
324.9793'034—dc22   2008026620

Printed in the United States of America

www.ballantinebooks.com

2 4 6 8 9 7 5 3

Book design by Liz Cosgrove

Dedicated to Kelton, Kennedy,
and O'Keeffe

Contents

★ ★ ★

Ms. Cahill
for
Congress

The Decision

★ ★ ★ ★ ★ ★ ★ ★ ★ ★ ★ ★ ★ ★ ★ ★ ★ ★ ★ ★

It seemed like just another afternoon at school. As I looked out at my class that September day in 1999, I pondered how to engage them. I knew that unless I got my sixth-grade students excited about ancient Greece, they would look upon the unit as a boring lesson about a bunch of dead people in togas. So I launched into a passionate discourse about how ancient Greece established the first democracy, one that our founding fathers had looked to when establishing our government. After explaining the differences between America's representative democracy and the Greek model of direct democracy, I moved on to the great Athenian general Pericles, who believed that if you don't participate in your representative government, you have no place in society.

At the back of the class, Heather, a quiet brown-haired girl well respected by her classmates, raised her hand.

"Well, that may have been fine for the Greeks, Ms. Cahill," she announced. "But you can't run for office in this country unless you're a millionaire or you know a lot of millionaires."

Wow, she's already figured that out at age twelve, I thought. *How sad.*

I, too, felt that if you're not wealthy, you don't really have a way to participate meaningfully in this country's political system. But it wasn't my role as a teacher to pass on my personal views.

"That's not exactly true," I countered. "All citizens in our country have the right to run for office. Would having a million dollars make things easier? I'm sure it would. But not having the money isn't going to prevent someone from being able to run."

I became so wrapped up in cheerleading for democracy, I neglected to think three steps ahead. I should have seen the next comment coming. Sixth graders are renowned for daring each other.

"Well, then, why don't you prove it, Ms. Cahill?" Heather challenged. "Why don't you run for office? You're a fair person, you're funny, you'd be great."

After a moment of uncomfortable silence during which I couldn't manage to spit out an answer, the rest of the class took up the idea and added their voices to Heather's. "Yeah!" and "Why don't you?" and "That'd be awesome!" rose up from the students like a wave.

Are you kidding me? I thought in a panic.

Of course, Heather was showing the kind of initiative I tried so hard to encourage. Just a month into the school year, my new students had already started to take over the classroom walls. My classroom was always bare at the beginning of the year with the exception of a few of my favorite posters, including the one that reads "You Can Change the World" and my "Cahill Hall of Fame" banner that always adorns a bulletin board. But now their art and writing projects enriched the space. Montages they had made about themselves hung from the ceiling over their desks. Butcher paper for ever-changing murals spanned the length of the back wall above the bright yellow countertops and kids' cubbyholes. "Your class would be about the worst place in the world for ADD kids," joked a friend of mine who's also a teacher. "They would never be able to pay attention to anything because there's so much stuff hanging everywhere." But I preferred an interactive room, where children learned through immersion.

I also worked to make it a democratic place. I believe in giving students choices. If I'm going to make students come up with a project to show me that they understand a math concept, they always have options because I know that kids—like the rest of us—have different learning styles. Not every person is an auditory learner. Some are visual, while others—including the one out of every ten or twelve who is ADD—are kinesthetic. You've got to be able to let them learn in ways that are going to make sense to them.

Unfortunately, many teachers will teach the way *they* learn best and most teachers are school nerds. We were usually the ones who sat in the front row because we wanted to be "the good students." We liked school because we did school very well. That's why we came back as adults; we get the game. But not everybody does. So as a teacher, I vary my approach to—and presentation of—the material in order to reach all these different kids because only about 20 percent of them learn the way I do. Students should be encouraged to do their best, not to fit into a mold that may not be suited to them.

I also want my kids to be able to speak up and talk to me about how they feel. If they don't like the way our spelling test is conducted, they have to explain why.

"I don't mind if you have a problem, but come to me with a solution, too," I say. "If you have a better way of doing things, that's fine, tell me. But if you're just coming to complain, I don't want to hear it."

This was especially important when it came to my sixth graders' social interactions on the playground. There was often drama after lunch recess, and they needed to learn how to be problem solvers, not whiners.

My students quickly became very vocal little people who excelled at giving one another feedback and thinking for themselves. We were a community of learners. I loved that. I also loved the fact that Heather had challenged my statement. But now I owed them an answer.

Looking at twenty-eight intent faces, I knew that I had just been handed a test. Would this grown-up be as contradictory and hypocritical as so many of the adults and personalities in their lives? If our country worked the way I had said it did, and if normal people could—and should—be involved in government, then as their teacher I shouldn't have a problem stepping up to do what they'd asked. It was as if they were saying, "Either you are what you say you are and you believe that whole line you gave us, or you're totally full of crap, and we're going to find out right now." In many ways, our roles of teacher and pupil had suddenly switched.

What I say is really going to matter, and I'd better think fast, I realized.

Thoughts rocketed through my brain like simultaneous fireworks explosions.

Oh my god, what have I gotten myself into?

Do I believe what I told them? Or am I simply a mouth-

piece for the establishment? Are these kids going to look back and resent me someday when they think about their teacher's rosy, half-honest introduction to politics?

How the hell can I run for office? I'm a divorced mom with three little kids. I have no money. I don't even own a house.

If I say no, will that prove their worst suspicions about people and the world around them?

This is crazy. I have no time, no influence, and absolutely no political connections. The only Kennedy I'm in good with is my daughter Kennedy.

This could be the best civics lesson ever!

Geez, what would my principal say?

There's no way I can do this.

This would be so cool for the kids! Why can't I do it?

How many adults whom these kids look up to wind up disappointing them? I don't want to be one of them.

Maybe she's right; maybe I should run.

As I looked at Heather's face, I realized that we ask children all the time to be brave. We ask them to be leaders, to say no to peer pressure, to turn down drugs, to step away from the crowd, and to be unafraid to take on challenges. We're really good at expecting that kind of courage from children, but how often do they see adults step up? How often do we actually model that you can do or be anything you want in life?

I had to buy myself some time. Smiling to hide my terror, I asked the kids for twenty-four hours, explaining that I needed to sleep on it since the decision would impact not only me but also my family.

"I knew she wouldn't do it," I heard a boy mutter.

Don't say I won't do something, a small voice inside me said. Anytime I'm told I won't—or can't—do something, a huge, ornery part of me answers, *Oh really? Wanna bet?*

Obstinacy is part of me. My dad, an engineer, probably fostered that beast. When I was little, he pushed me to be athletic and outgoing, to climb trees, to work on cars. I can remember him teaching me how to play with gears, do woodworking, and build things. He pressed me to not get pigeonholed into typical female roles, and he treated me more like a boy than his little girl. Even though my parents had divorced by the time I was a teenager, both he and my mother demanded that I pursue a college education so I'd always be able to take care of myself and be independent— they never wanted me to need a man. I love them for that.

We grew up without TV; my father did not want our brains turned to mush. He preferred that we spend our time reading, playing outside, or doing something else of value. At dinner, we sat and actually had discussions, ones in which you were expected to have an opinion. And you had better be able to defend it.

My parents were basically hippies who ate organic and never kept white flour or white sugar in the house. They had walked for McGovern and made buttons for him out of leather, and they had supported Cesar Chavez. My midwestern father's political evolution took place in the navy while stationed at Treasure Island just off of San Francisco. My mother owed her liberal politics in part to her own parents, who believed that the nation's direction is determined by its leadership and that the Republicans would prove the demise of this country. In my maternal grandmother's front room, a huge picture of the pope on one side of the mantel was balanced by an even larger picture of JFK on the other. The family joke was that if you didn't become a nun or marry a Kennedy, you had to go into public service and do something meaningful with your life that would give back to society.

Grandma's compassionate outlook, however, did not extend to Republicans, whom she believed to be basically evil to the core (or simply outright stupid), selfish, and mean-spirited. She particularly despised Ronald Reagan. My grandfather, a drummer in the swing era who once met Ella Fitzgerald, had known him from college and thought he was a womanizing drunk. My grandma simply called him a rotten son of a bitch.

The older she got, the more cantankerous she became. I was in eighth grade when Reagan was shot. I can remember being sent home from school that day. Even though he was not on the list of heroes I had been taught to admire, I still felt reverence for the presidency and concern for President Reagan and his family. As soon as I walked into my grandma's house after getting off the bus, I announced, "Grandma! The President's been shot!" She angrily fired back, "If I had shot him, at least I would have made sure to kill the rotten son of a bitch!"

"Grandma, my god!" I yelped. "Monsignor would not approve of all that hatred. And isn't it illegal to threaten to kill the President?"

My words did nothing to lessen her hatred of Reagan in particular and Republicans in general. They stood squarely against her beliefs that as a country we had an ethical duty and a responsibility to care for those less fortunate. She felt that a country's true character was proven by how the poor, elderly, and those too weak to care for themselves were treated within that society. And since I grew up with the blessing of "grandma care" rather than day care, those attitudes rubbed off on me.

My grandparents lived what they preached. They cared for my great-grandmother in her eighties, my great-aunt in her late seventies, and their own grown daughter after a terrible car accident cost her a leg and left her with permanent severe brain damage. All three of their charges were in wheelchairs. Then they took in and raised their five- and seven-year-old grandchildren, who had been in the car accident with their mother and suffered horrible trauma. With my parents divorcing, they also took care of my sister and me every day while our mother worked.

In my eyes, Grandma and Grandpa were saints. They never complained about the situation they were in, although I know they suffered through many difficult days and nights. I can remember watching my grandpa seated at his card table working on a jigsaw puzzle and chewing on his cigar. Monsignor Gallagher would come to the house to give mass to all of the people in wheelchairs. Grandma would eagerly serve him coffee, and Grandpa would encourage him to tell stories because they loved to hear his Irish accent. Every now and then Grandpa would mention that this was not the postretirement life he had anticipated. He had wanted to take my grandma on a trip to New England to see the fall colors and to visit historic places he'd read about. But then the accident happened and four generations of people were now struggling to live together.

Though I came from a very progressive family, I wasn't prepared for the diversity I encountered in college. When my dad drove me from our home in Reno, Nevada, to the University of New Mexico, which is one-third Anglo, one-third Hispanic, and one-third Native American, one of the football players hanging out by the dorm greeted me with, "Yo, baby, what's happenin'? What's your name?"

Unnerved, I snapped, "What? Don't 'Yo baby' me. I don't know you. Who do you think you are, talking to me like that?"

He and his buddies cracked up at this white girl so obviously from a hick town. Though I was annoyed by the forwardness of his greeting, I was equally embarrassed by my reaction, which had been triggered by discomfort.

Living in the dorms was like being in the United Nations, and the more I heard about my fellow students' experiences growing up in places like Detroit, Los Angeles, and New York, the more I realized that they came from a world I had never experienced. My grandparents were poor Irish Catholics. They talked to me endlessly about not being able to get jobs, being called cat-lickers (a derogatory slang term for Roman *Catholics*), and having rocks thrown at them while growing up in Des Moines, Iowa. Grandpa had had a cross burned on his lawn. In the Midwest during those years, people hated the Catholics as much as they hated the Irish, and they hated the Irish Catholics most of all. "You better be proud about who you are because we fought long and hard to assimilate into this country," my grandparents insisted. Until I got to college, however, I never considered what it must be like for people who couldn't assimilate because of race.

Active in campus politics from the start, I soon joined the Black student union. Admittedly that was a weird choice for a white girl, but a class in African-American history had spun my head. We learned that the industrial revolution and southern agricultural wealth never would have materialized without free labor from African Americans. Lectures and the course text *Before the Mayflower: A History of Black America* by Lerone Bennett Jr. also chronicled groundbreaking African-American accomplishments I had never heard of—accomplishments that had proven critical to the development and evolution of the country. I can remember thinking, *Wait a minute—I took tons of history classes in high school and read anything I could get my hands on, and I don't remember hearing any of this.* I actually confronted my professor one day at the end of class.

"Either you are lying or my textbooks lied to me all through school."

Dr. Cortez Williams just laughed at me.

I began reexamining everything in my life. Much of what I'd taken for granted no longer seemed fair. I had attended Reno High, a U.S. Department of Education Blue Ribbon School that was also listed among the nation's top high schools. I had assumed that most schools were like mine, only to learn from books like Jonathan Kozol's *Savage Inequalities: Children in America's Schools* about the dilapidated condition of many inner-city schools, where ceilings leaked, toilets didn't work, and supplies were nonexistent. How did we expect the students in those schools to feel— and act—like valued members of society when every non-verbal message said that they weren't? What message did we convey when those same children took buses to faraway schools to compete athletically, where they saw beautiful facilities where everything worked and, which, by the way, were predominantly white?

When I started dating my future husband, Lamont, a charismatic, caramel-skinned African American from the inner city who didn't smoke or drink and who has still never touched a drug, all those issues of race and class became part of my life. If he was going to get pulled over and harassed by police, I would be in that car. In addition, I could now penetrate African-American society. Dinner parties and bridal showers provided me a firsthand view into an amazingly rich and layered culture that I was totally unfamiliar with. I learned to admire a great deal about African-American families: the way they use humor to deal with sadness or disappointment, the way women band together and support each other, the huge extended families. Sure, I saw some black males (along with many in the white community) struggling with alcohol and other drugs. When they couldn't get a job, some of those guys did things that weren't good for them. Still, I began to pay especially close attention to the media's disturbing portrayal of black men as an endangered species, because I certainly didn't want that sentence for the man I already knew I would marry or for any sons we might have.

Yearning for a way to impact a world that I increasingly saw as inequitable, I considered going into civil rights law. Finally Dr. Williams, the professor I had challenged and to whom I had grown quite close, said, "As a civil rights attorney, you'll be reacting to situations that have already happened. You won't help change anything. Since you obviously don't care about making a lot of money [civil rights law not being known for bringing in massive earnings], why don't you think about becoming a teacher?"

Upon reflection, I realized that instead of helping a few people each year by asking the court to uphold the law, I'd be able to reach a class of thirty kids annually. Perhaps by teaching them to be more tolerant and to recognize and appreciate the differences among all of us, I could make things better. Being proactive and preventing tragedy, rather than dwelling on it, struck me as a much more positive way to live my life. So I decided to teach.

Lamont and I married directly out of college and had a son right away, which nixed our dreams of getting into the Peace Corps. Instead, in the fall of 1990, we moved to West Covina, California, to work in the inner city. Lamont took a job counseling kids in the juvenile justice system in La Verne. He would help them with everything from communication skills to how to present themselves outside the ghetto. I taught a combined kindergarten/first-grade class at a private school in Compton, where I was the only white teacher they'd ever had.

I had never been the "only one" before. I had never walked into a restaurant and had people scrutinize me up and down with that "Hmm, who does she think she is?" look or gone into a department store that had no white people in it. I had never been targeted with overt racism, and I still smart over a mother who marched her kid out of my classroom and to the principal, announcing, "That white bitch will *not* be teaching my child—you find another room for him." It made me better understand what my then-husband experienced daily. But I hated living in Los Angeles and couldn't wait to get back to a smaller, less congested, and less polluted town. I didn't want to raise my infant son in a place that I felt was systemically unhealthy.

The following year, we returned to New Mexico and bought a 2,500-square-foot, four-bedroom house. Lamont took a job teaching social skills to—and running employ-ability workshops for—Job Corps teenagers and I opened a preschool. Just three years later our marriage failed, and I made the decision to leave my successful preschool business and return to Reno with our children, including our newborn, to care for my father, who was dying of cancer. I was devastated that my marriage hadn't worked out; running home felt safe. I figured that Reno would be a nurturing community in which to raise my kids. Besides, I owed it to my father, a wild man who lived by the seat of his pants and whom I adored. I had chosen to live with him during my teenage years after he and my mom divorced, so this man who had given up being an engineer to run his own organic barbecue restaurant had basically raised me.

My dad died before I had actually managed to relocate, but I moved anyway. The decision was very emotional and equally illogical, since I hadn't found a job and missed my old work life. My preschool provided a wonderfully creative outlet where I could teach in a way that was educationally valuable and socially responsible. Each month's theme reflected the multicultural background of my diverse clientele, so we learned about Native American, Jewish, African, and Hispanic art, food, stories, and music. The preschool, which was quite profitable, was popular among those doctors, lawyers, and professors who wanted their kids to learn about many different backgrounds in an environment where their own culture would be honored. Had I stayed, I would have expanded the program and taken in more students. But I wanted to walk away from everything that had gone wrong in New Mexico and find a new life.

I knew I would be fine in Reno. And I was right. Though my father's will giving me his house was successfully disputed in court by his wife, despite their ongoing divorce proceedings during his illness, I secured a teaching job with a single e-mail to a school principal. I would teach kindergarten at a private Christian school. And while $8 an hour would be difficult to live on, the school agreed to pay me to do my student teaching that fall as long as I promised to stay for the whole year. I was fortunate to have fallen into such an arrangement, although I had a hard time being surrounded by "good Christians" who were so politically conservative. Those two characteristics seemed so diametrically opposed. The disdain for Catholics was equally difficult to take, but I needed the work so I tried to keep my mouth shut as much as possible.

Though my husband probably would have preferred to

stay in New Mexico, he moved to Reno as well so that we could share custody of our three children. The arrangement was ideal, since I saw his tremendous involvement with our children as essential for their emotional development. Joint custody, however, meant no child support, since we each had the kids half the time. We split the doctors' bills, but otherwise we were responsible for our own expenses. My solution—to work a second and third job once I landed a teaching position in a public school—cost me physically, but I needed the money. I was willing to trade sleep for a safety net that, even at the best of times, could barely hold me and my children.

Accepting my class's dare to run for office could rip a gaping hole in that net. Running for public office would inevitably compound my overloaded schedule. But I approached teaching with a sense of tremendous responsibility, and too much was at stake not to seriously consider the proposition.

I realized that this was one of those defining challenges that life throws our way. Driving home from school the day my students dropped their bombshell, I tried to talk it over with my kids—O'Keeffe, then 5, Kennedy, 6, and Kelton, 9—since a decision to run would affect them too. I figured that I might encourage more discussion if I broached the topic informally in the car, rather than convening a family meeting at home.

"What would you think if I ran for office?" I asked.

They were so young, they weren't even sure what running for office meant.

"Well, you know what the president is, and you know what an election is. What would you think if I did that?"

They didn't react at first. They still didn't understand. Eventually, they would decide that living in the White House once I was elected president would be awesome. I never even tried to set them straight.

That night, I continued to wrestle with myself. I worried about mudslinging and how "dirty" politics might affect me, my family, and my school. But mostly I worried about where I'd find the time. To make ends meet, I was already working three nights a week as a cocktail waitress at a local Irish pub, while high school kids babysat my children or the kids were with my ex. I went in at six and worked until 2 a.m. Some nights I didn't get home until four in the morning. After only a couple hours of sleep, I headed back to the classroom ready to drop. Still, on good nights I came home with as much as $150. Over the course of the year, that meant an additional five or six grand. Selling real estate on the occasional weekend added another three to seven thousand a year if I was lucky. That was how we got by.

I had every reason to decline my students' challenge. Still, I was drawn to the project. We teachers talk about education needing to be more real-world, so kids absorb what they're being taught. Instead of solely teaching them math facts with "kill-and-drill" worksheets that focus so much on repetition they extinguish all enthusiasm for learning, for example, you have them build a birdhouse where they actually have to measure and calculate angles. Studies on best practices for classroom instruction have repeatedly said that it's imperative for students to find relevance in their curriculum. So how about running a political campaign? That's pretty darn authentic and could be made extremely pertinent.

I also considered what Heather had said. *Maybe she's right,* I thought. *Maybe we do need working-class folks to run for office, because I can't think of any elected officials with that kind of background. What if the check-out gal at the gro-*

cery ran for office? What if my mailman ran? How great would that be?

My dad used to talk about how to bring the common man into government. "I wish political office was more like the jury system," he'd say. "What if instead of the elitists running this country trying to pretend that they know how we're living, you got a notice in the mail that said, 'As part of this society, it's your turn to serve two years in the House of Representatives. Housing in Washington will be provided.'" Wow, that would shake things up!

Wasn't that how this country was supposed to be run? Yet even the political leaders who started this country came from the privileged class. Thomas Jefferson, with his slaves in Monticello, wasn't exactly down with the people. Our country has never lived up to being "of the people, by the people, and for the people." The idea of running a true grassroots campaign was appealing. And though naïve, I was rash enough to think that I could do it.

My boyfriend at the time—a charming, good-looking man with green eyes, a chiseled nose and chin, and a mean streak when he drank, which was often—disagreed with me.

"That sounds ridiculous," Derrick said over the phone. "I hope you're not really going to do that. You'll only embarrass yourself."

Okay, honey, thanks for the support, I thought to myself, unaware that I would soon face a number of increasingly vicious comments about me, my children, and my political aspirations. In my home, Kelton, Kennedy, and O'Keeffe know that there are ways to argue fairly, and unwritten relationship rules that you don't violate with verbal attacks. That's how I was raised, and I made sure to bring up my children the same way. Derrick understood none of those boundaries.

I hadn't seen his ugly side during the first year we dated. He took me on trips to Mexico and Hawaii. Being so destitute, it felt good to have a man nineteen years my senior spoil me with gifts, dinners, and attention. He was very outdoorsy like my dad, who had hunted and fished, and I liked that as well. And having worked for years in the federal court system as a judge's clerk, he hung out with people like the mayor of Las Vegas. I was impressed by who he knew, as well as how many people he knew.

The first time he blew up at me over dinner and margaritas during a fishing trip, I slept on the hotel floor and refused to talk to him for days after we got back home. "I'm so sorry. I guess I drank too much," he said. "I shouldn't talk to you that way." Eventually, ongoing apologies and flowers convinced me to go out to dinner with him. Another few dinners and we were seeing each other again.

I didn't know it then, but a pattern had been established. We would have a good time until the next blowup, which once he was sober was always followed by tender apologies about how he would understand if I left because he knew I deserved better. Part of me thought I could fix him and change this dynamic. And after being stuck at home raising three little kids on no money, his on-the-go lifestyle seemed like an escape from my depressing post-divorce sentence. He knew many prestigious people so we went to lots of swanky events. After working so hard and barely making it, having fun was a pleasure, even if I had to pay the price now and then when he got drunk.

By the time I had seen the full extent of his vile temper and habits, getting away from him was like getting out of a bowl of spaghetti. He owned the house I rented. His name was on my car loan. "I'll take your fucking car," he threatened when I talked about leaving. "Then how will you drive those kids around?" It would take a year and a half of planning to finally extricate myself from the relationship four years later.

Still, by 1999 I was already used to his degradation. If anything, his reaction cemented a decision I didn't even know I had made.

Of course, I couldn't make a move without my principal's consent. I called her that night. I liked—and deeply respected—Penny LaBranch. She was middle class and proud of it, yet she exuded class and dignity. She drove a '57 Chevy with a license plate that read "57 Lady." Her husband, a mechanic, owned his own garage and Penny handled his bookkeeping. Unlike other administrators, she seemed real to me. If I had a meeting with parents who made excuses for their child's behavior instead of holding the kid accountable, she smiled and put on a show for them. But as soon as they left, she'd say, "Shut the door." Once the door was safely closed, she would ask, "Was that the biggest load of crap you ever heard in your life?" And I would crack up. She always backed her teachers, and she believed in us. But she was demanding because she wanted the best for the children in her school. If we teachers weren't doing the right thing for the students, look out!

Penny could be difficult to work for, but I knew she would never ask me to do something she wasn't willing to do herself. She even showed up at school every now and then in shorts and a T-shirt to weed the flower beds or wipe down tables in the cafeteria. Nor was it unusual to see her picking up trash on the playground. Some instructors thought she expected too much of teachers. I even heard of a few who were terrified to interview with her because they had heard that before the interview she would go out to the parking lot and look in their car to see if they were neat. The rumor wasn't true, but it was funny.

Penny was less supportive than usual over the course of this conversation.

"I don't know, Tierney. You know there's this huge push to meet the state standards. You have to teach to the test and address those standards in the curriculum. We're all under the gun here, administrators and teachers. We both know that's not good teaching. It's horseshit. But that's the direction things are going."

On the other end of the line, I heard what I'm sure were ice cubes clinking in a glass.

"How's this going to look?" she asked.

I couldn't answer her because the same thought had crossed my mind. I knew I was going to agree to run because of the project's enormous educational value and because I didn't want kids to throw in the towel at age twelve. They were already resigned to the notion that unless your dad is a Kennedy or a Bush, you're screwed; you might as well give up and get a job at Wal-Mart. If I had to be the instrument to prove that assumption wrong, I was good with that.

"So how do we do this and not get you in trouble?" she finally asked.

I could tell that she had come around and that she wouldn't oppose my decision to run. Though we didn't manage to answer her question that evening, I knew I had her in my corner.

With Penny's tacit agreement still echoing in the phone, I called my mom, who made it clear that she thought my running for office was yet another one of my idealistic and impractical ideas. My mother truly adores me, but she fretted about me to no end in those days. Though she believed in me, she knew how close to the edge I teetered most of the time, and worried that my tendency to overachieve would push me off that edge.

"Are you kidding?" she said. "You can hardly handle the life you're living. And you want to add one more thing? You won't be able to manage."

I love my mom, but I hate anyone telling me that I'm not capable. That pissed me off. My poor mother. Whenever she tried to protect her strong-willed daughter, I assumed that she doubted my abilities and had to prove her wrong. *Just watch me,* I thought ever so typically. *I'll show you.*

I knew there would be challenges, but they seemed manageable. When it came down to it, I figured that running for office wouldn't be such a big deal. *I'll get my name on the ballot; the class will research how to do that. Then I'll get clobbered in the primaries and it'll be over. I'll have done what the kids asked me to do, and I'll have proved a point. Plus, just think what they'll learn.*

The following morning, I delivered my verdict to my class. "I will accept your challenge and agree to run for office, on one condition. My challenge to you is that as a class you will run this campaign." A cheer went up.

I was beyond excited. I had them in a place where they cared. They would be driving the curriculum, with their choices leading us on our journey of discovery. I knew this campaign would generate passionate curiosity. Deep inside I've always known that that's how education should be, for therein lies the richest learning.

My choice to run, however, would cost me in ways I had never imagined. Had I known what I was in for, I almost certainly would never have agreed to do it.

2

Getting Started

★ ★ ★ ★ ★ ★ ★ ★ ★ ★ ★ ★ ★ ★ ★ ★ ★ ★ ★ ★

Reno hunkers along Nevada's western border in a long, dry, slender valley known as Truckee Meadows. The city of more than 210,000 residents is bordered to the west by foothills and to the east by rounded and mostly bare brown rises where wild mustangs still roam. The hills were once forested with pines and piñons, but many of the trees were felled to shore up mine shafts once silver was discovered in 1859, eleven years after Nevada had been officially acquired from Mexico. Until then, the area had served largely as a way station for people rushing to strike gold in California. The discovery of the rich gold and especially silver veins known as the Comstock Lode, located twenty-five miles from Reno, prompted people to flock to one of the nation's last frontiers. Twenty years later, in what would become a boom-and-bust pattern for Reno, the local mines seemingly petered out, and the newfound population disappeared as quickly as it had materialized. Some did stay. Descendants of those Irish and Italian prospectors and Basque sheepherders still live here today. A second round of gold, silver, and this time copper strikes around 1900 lured a new wave of inhabitants as well as the expansion of the railroad—a boon to the ranchers and farmers who had slowly settled the area. With a train and a river running smack through the middle of the city, the town became a transportation hub.

Though Nevada still produces 11 percent of the world's gold, Reno experienced its second bust at the end of World War I, when the demand for its mines' minerals dried up. The city reinvented itself in 1930 by shortening the time required to obtain a divorce, thereby attracting a new, highly transient population of socialites and celebrities looking to sever the ties of matrimony as quickly and painlessly as possible. Divorce ranches sprang up. The new source of revenue brought a new identity. Instead of saying that you were getting divorced, you simply said you were heading to Reno for a vacation.

The following year, gambling was legalized in Nevada, and Reno soon became known as the gambling capital of the world—or "Sin City"—a title it would hold until the creation of Las Vegas. The body count created by the droves of tourists abandoning Reno for Vegas is now evident downtown. Failed casinos, long in the tooth, are being converted into condos, while old, boarded-up motels and sorry downtown trailer parks attest to better days. Still, three hundred days of sun annually, year-round sports, and glittering new casinos draw hundreds of thousands of tourists a year.

But Reno doesn't rely only on tourism. The city, which like the rest of Nevada has no corporate income tax and no franchise tax on corporations, has attracted new industry, notably warehousing and distribution. That, in turn, has helped spark the latest housing boom, which has earned Reno/Sparks the designation of most overvalued housing market in the country. Despite that dubious distinction,

Reno's population has grown by over 20 percent in the last ten years.

For all its warts, I love Reno. Though I didn't move here full-time until my freshman year of high school, I've always considered it my home in a way that I've never thought of Sacramento, where I spent my childhood. As a teenager, I lived here with my father in a tiny cream-colored two-bedroom house located in one of the established elm-shaded neighborhoods west of Virginia Avenue, the city's unofficial dividing line. Despite being on the "good" side of town and in a neighborhood populated by professionals, the houses near us were also modest.

This unassuming pocket, however, was—and still is—flanked by estates that sit up on the bluff and overlook the Truckee River. Every morning I'd walk past mansions with white picket fences surrounding lawns upon which horses could have grazed, cut across an empty lot four blocks from my house, and run down a hill that drops into the creek by my award-winning school.

So many famous people have come out of Reno High—including U.S. Senator Patrick Anthony McCarrran (1897), Nevada State Architect Frederic Joseph DeLongchamps (1900), U.S. Congressman Walter S. Baring, Jr. (1929), actress Dawn Wells (1956), New York Giants (NFL) head coach Ray Handley (1962), and major league baseball pitcher Shawn Boskie (1985)—that the Piazzo brothers, owners of a big sporting-goods store in town, who used to be Reno High students themselves, built an alumni hall of fame on the high school campus.

Reno has it all as far as I'm concerned—great weather, beautiful neighborhoods with tree-lined streets, terrific schools, a top-notch university (University of Nevada, Reno), tons of sports and recreation, and plenty of culture and entertainment. Artistic offerings range from the Nevada Museum of Art, featuring traveling exhibits and local artists, to museums that showcase the incredible Harrah's car collection, as well as slot machines and gun collections. If you're a local, you don't usually head to the casinos unless there's a show or an event you want to see. But the performances are big draws for tourists and locals alike.

Reno is a city of contrasts. You can kayak, swim, golf, play tennis, ski, and snowshoe, often on the same day if you've got the stamina. If you drive half an hour, you can jump into a high mountain lake or, if you go east, find yourself in the middle of the Black Rock Desert. And though we actually live in the high desert, rich irrigated ranch land still abounds to the south.

The city's diversity isn't restricted to geography. You see it economically and you see it socially. And since public schools are a snapshot of the society from which they draw, nowhere do you see it more clearly than in the classroom. At Sarah Winnemucca Elementary School, I always had students from the Eastern European bloc, Thailand, Japan, and China, along with Latino, African-American, and Anglo kids. I'd even get a sprinkling of students from places like Uganda. Some kids came from low-income housing, others from parents who were involved with the casinos (one Bulgarian student's father was a circus artist who performed downtown at Circus Circus) or with the University of Nevada, Reno, and still others from families who regularly vacationed abroad and whose children's monthly allowances probably equaled my car payment. I loved having kids whose parents came from all walks of life and from all kinds of nationalities and ethnicities. And I loved the fact that the campaign we were about to launch would be managed by a group that actually reflected the electorate's diversity.

Of course now that I had agreed to run, my students needed to decide what office I would seek. Naturally, they wanted me to run for president.

"President of what?" Penny asked when I told her.

As it turns out, I wasn't old enough.

"The constitution says you have to be thirty-five years old," I told my students the following morning. "I'm only thirty-three. I can't be president."

"How about vice president?" they asked.

I giggled at the thought of running for VP.

"No, it doesn't work that way. You don't run for the office of vice president independently. It's not a separate election. You are actually asked to be a presidential candidate's running mate, and I am pretty sure that neither George [Bush] nor Al [Gore] are going to be calling anytime soon."

They still looked confused, so I explained that each candidate picks a running mate based on what they believe will make the best ticket.

"What's a ticket?" Jordan, who lived for basketball, asked.

"It's like being a team of two that's going to face off with another team of two in a contest," I said. "So why would a presidential candidate pick a particular running mate?"

"Because they're friends," Elyse said.

"Let's see if that really makes sense," I countered. "If Jenny picks Sam because he's her best friend, does that give her the best opportunity to win? Maybe, maybe not. It would depend on how the voters felt about Sam. When we're talking about the United States, we also need to think of the electoral college and how many electoral votes a state has to offer, and what states a candidate needs to win. For example, Bill Clinton picked Al Gore to be his running mate. They were both Southerners, which meant they would do well in the Southern states. But he also might have chosen him because Al was more popular in certain states that Bill needed to win."

"Oh, so it's sort of a mathematical decision in order to get the most electoral votes?" asked Ingrid.

"Yep," I said. "That's usually what it's about. It's marketing."

We moved on.

"Okay, what's the next most-powerful position?" asked Jamie.

"Let me draw some pictures with my very untalented artistic abilities and we'll look at sort of an outline of power. You have the president and the vice president. Then you have the Speaker of the House and the President Pro Tempore of the Senate (who happens to be the VP). He's an equal to the Speaker of the House, and breaks ties in the Senate if there are any."

"Can you be Speaker of the House?" asked Sam, a very well-rounded student who was greatly admired at recess for his basketball prowess.

It was clear that they weren't going to let me run for dogcatcher or city council. With sixth graders, everything's a contest. It's always about the biggest, the best, the fastest. Wanting me to go for the shiniest brass ring possible, they were now running through the pecking order, using their evolving knowledge of the three branches of government as their guide.

"Nope, you can't run for that either," I said. "The Speaker of the House is actually a member of the House. He or she ran for office just like all the other Congresspeople, but then has managed to be elected by his or her peers to a leadership role. Probably one of the most important sidebars here is that the Speaker's party—Democrat or Republican—has to have the majority in the House. Say we divided the class up for kickball and the team with the most players got to pick one of their teammates to organize the kickball tournament. That person would then be in charge of making sure the rules were followed, and would also have an opportunity to vote."

Having agreed that according to the Constitution there was no way I was going to be able to run for president, and explored why vice president, Speaker of the House, and President Pro Tem were all out as well, we got to the House and the Senate. I drew a big rectangular building with a dome on top of it.

"One side of this building is called the House, the other side the Senate," I said. "What's the building called?"

"The Capitol building," a male voice shouted as I faced the whiteboard, writing down whatever was yelled out at me.

Another child disagreed. "I thought it was the Congress building!"

"It's not called that, it's called the Congressional building," another yelled.

"Okay, well I've heard it called the Congressional building and the Capitol building," I said. "So let's talk about the two groups that use this building. What's the purpose of the House and the Senate?"

Heather chimed in with the observation that they make up the legislative branch of our government. I backed up to make sure everyone else was following along.

"How many branches of government do we have? Three? Do you all agree?"

"Yes! We learned that last year, Ms. Cahill."

"Okay, so what are the three branches of government? We know there's a legislative branch; you've already told me that."

"There's the presidential branch," shouted Sam.

"Sort of, but what's its proper name?"

"Oh, the executive branch," Frank, a bashful boy who often looked up at the ceiling when he spoke to me, informed the class.

"Right. How about the third branch?"

This took a little bit more contemplation. Finally Rocket, whose mother was a sixth-grade teacher at a different school, shouted, "The judicial branch. The judges, they balance it." Rocket was always good for a quick clarification.

"What was that?" I asked. "Tell me more."

"Well, the three branches are supposed to keep each other in check so no one branch goes crazy with power."

"How would that work, Rocket?"

"Well, the legislative branch makes laws, the judicial branch decides whether they are constitutional, and the president gets to be the boss, but he can't violate the constitution either. The other two branches keep him in line."

"Anyone else have anything they'd like to add?"

No one else did. "Okay, so let's go back to the House and the Senate," I said. "If they're both part of the legislative branch, how are they different and why do we need two bodies within the legislative branch?"

Rocket eagerly shared that the Senate had one hundred members, two from each state.

"The House has more people, but I don't know how many," offered Ingrid, a very bright Nordic-looking child with almost white hair and stunning sky-blue eyes whose mother was a social worker and father a geologist. I'd been to their home for dinner, and they had a happy household, including two Great Danes who were as much a part of the family as Ingrid and her sister were.

"Why does it have more people?" I asked.

"I think it has to do with how big a state is," Ingrid replied.

Rocket quickly corrected her. "Actually it's not how big the state itself is, but how populated it is."

"Good job, Rocket and Ingrid. So does anyone know how many people there are in the House?"

Frank hurried over to the computer to find the answer. "Four hundred thirty-five!" he announced, clearly proud of himself.

"So do we know how many we have from Nevada?"

Within seconds, Frank notified the class that our state has three representatives. "Shelley Berkley is the congress-woman from Vegas, then there's Jim Gibbons, and there's a new third district in the Henderson area of southern Nevada."

"So is a congressman or senator more important?" asked Ingrid. "Or are they equal in power?"

Never one to provide an answer if the kids could figure it out on their own, I replied, "What do you guys think?"

Frank jumped in. I couldn't believe how he was asserting himself. "Well I think that senators have more power since there are fewer of them. Fewer usually means more scarce and therefore the less you have probably the more valuable it is."

"Who agrees with that?" I asked.

The kids nodded, some agreeing out loud.

Yup, they had definitely gotten the supply-and-demand concept. Being one out of a hundred definitely makes you more important than being one out of 435.

"I think you should run for the Senate," said Ingrid.

"Does anyone know who our current senators are?"

Computer guru Frank quickly found the information. "We have a guy named Harry Reid and another guy named Richard Bryan."

"Well, the Senate goes up for reelection every six years.

Frank, can you tell if one of those seats will be available to run for?"

Frank couldn't find the answer right away, but eventually came across an article saying that Bryan was stepping down to retire. The news electrified the entire class.

"Okay, let's run for the Senate then," I said.

"Yes! Yes! Yes!" the kids hollered.

Sixth graders crack me up. They're the big guys on campus since most elementary schools go from kindergarten through sixth grade, and they're in this very funny developmental stage. One day a student will bring a box of Tonka trucks to school and he'll be out in the playground building hills and roads, and he's a little boy. The next day he'll have his hat turned around backward and be asking a girl out. He might try to hold hands with a girl—that's a pretty big deal—or even take her behind the back steps and kiss her. But inevitably he'll go back to his Tonka trucks because that's safe. The girls will still skip rope and play hopscotch, but then they want to talk about the possibility of having a boyfriend. It's as if kids this age step one toe into the teenage world, find it uncomfortable, and then revert to being children for a bit. That dynamic goes back and forth, which drives their parents nuts.

"Oh my god!" a few said every single year. "I had this sane, wonderful child who's crazy now! I don't know what's going on with that kid!"

This campaign would compel my on-the-cusp students to rise to the occasion.

"Okay, then that's what we'll do," I told them. "We'll run for a seat in the U.S. Senate."

First, however, I had to win over the school district, since it has veto power over any classroom and extracurricular activity.

3

The Opposition

* * * * * * * * * * * * * * * * * * * *

"You know, as it turns out, I can't run for president," I told Penny when I went to see her at the end of the day. "I'm not old enough."

"Oh, thank god!"

She looked so relieved, I realized that she had misconstrued my comment.

"Oh, no, I'm still running. Just not for president. We're going to run for the Senate instead."

"Well, we had better get our ducks in a row then," she said with a small sigh. "Let me call some people down at the district and let's set up a meeting so that we don't get ourselves into a nasty situation that we can't get out of."

Within days, Penny and I crammed into her office along with Steve Mulvenon, then the district's communications director, responsible for handling media relations; Paul Dugan, the assistant superintendent; and Kathy Yapp, our school's vice principal. I expected flak about how this was going to fit with the mandate to teach to the standards.

Standards are requirements set by the state regarding

student performance. Math standard 1.6.1, for example, states that all sixth graders will be able to read, write, add, subtract, multiply, and divide with decimals, fractions, and percents. That's one standard. We probably have forty math standards in sixth grade. As a teacher, however, you're also responsible for making sure that every student can do all the standards from the fifth, fourth, third, second, and first grades because you're building on those skills.

The standards idea started with President Bill Clinton and the notion that schools and teachers should be more accountable and more consistent, so if you moved from one sixth grade in Florida to another one midyear in Oklahoma, all sixth graders would be learning the same kinds of things. The states set their curriculum standards. Local districts can choose to increase the rigor of those standards, which our district has done. The state standards are tied to standardized tests administered by the State Department of Education and used to judge schools through the Adequate Yearly Progress (AYP) test. This national push for quality control, now known as No Child Left Behind, is tied to money, since the federal government can disqualify a state for federal funds if it doesn't participate in yearly assessing. So the pressure on the states to comply is tremendous.

As a teacher, you not only need to know the standards inside and out, you need to be able to prove that you've taught them and that the child has mastered them. The resulting pre- and post-testing has turned the classroom into a testing environment rather than a learning environment. The whole thing nauseated me. Our vice principal brought us all these disgusting practice test booklets and expected us to get the kids to regurgitate the answers, and then test them again and again. Where's the growth in that? You're simply testing these kids to the point where they're never going to think for themselves.

Memorization in order to perform well on a standardized multiple-choice exam is not authentic teaching. Instead of helping build strong, effective citizens by figuring out all they've learned, you're trying to find out what they haven't. And instead of measuring mastery, comprehension and growth, all too often these tests include trick questions that require students to select the best answer from several partially correct options. "Aha! Gotcha!" That's horrid to me. I'd much rather find out what they know and teach to their strengths rather than try to ferret out their weaknesses.

I'm not saying that tests don't have their place. Teachers love to assess kids, and we find all kinds of ways to do it. But everyone learns at his or her own pace, and only 20 percent of students learn the traditional way. Our twenty-eighth president, Woodrow Wilson, could barely read until the sixth grade. Besides, some kids don't test well. To put so much pressure on one test is ridiculous.

Like all other fourth graders, my poor daughter—a very serious child who's the high achiever of the family—had to take the "biggie" test where the state scores are reported to the Department of Education in Washington, D.C. When she came to see me at recess that morning, I realized that her eyebrows had disappeared.

"Oh my god! Kennedy!" I cried out. "What is going on with you? What's happening? Your forehead is all red and your eyebrows are gone! What happened?"

Embarrassed, she muttered, "Um, they were itching and I just kept rubbing them."

"Rubbing them?" I asked. "Do you need Benadryl? Are you okay? What could have made them itch?"

"I don't know, I don't know."

When Kennedy returned to my classroom at the end of school, she had pulled out all her eyelashes as well.

I thought she was going crazy, so I took her to a doctor.

"Why is my child doing this?" I asked in a panic.

It turns out that many kids in high-stress situations will inflict this kind of damage on themselves.

"Kennedy, what is going on?" I inquired again and again.

My daughter is such a serious, quiet little thing that it's hard to get her to open up. Finally, she burst into tears.

"I'm so afraid of not going to the fifth grade, Mom."

"Wait a minute; you're going to the fifth grade. You have good grades."

"Yeah, but the test. The test is so important."

Her teacher had drilled into her students how critical it was for them to do well. As a result, they had gotten the impression that a bad grade would reflect on them, when we teachers are actually the ones who get graded. I was sickened. *This is so wrong,* I thought to myself. But since the federal funding that the state—and therefore the school district—receives is tied to performance on these tests, that's today's school environment. That's why my deviating from strictly teaching the standards was such a touchy proposition.

"Can you please address which standards you'll be teaching, how you'll be teaching them, and how you'll be assessing them?" Kathy, the school's vice principal, said as soon as the project had been explained.

I knew she would try to slam me. So I came to the meeting with copies of the state standards marked with colored Post-it tabs and annotated.

"Okay, so let's look at number one," I said.

I proceeded to march them through the curriculum requirements involving civics—which include studying U.S. government, and our country's political process and economic systems—showing how learning firsthand about the processes of government related. Both the assistant superintendent and the media relations guy were thrilled.

"This is awesome," they said, tacitly endorsing the project. "How do you foresee yourself running this campaign?"

"Well, I don't see it being worth anything at all unless the kids run it," I said. "This isn't for me. I'm not the one who wanted to run for office. I'm letting them vicariously live through me, so it's only right that they have a say in everything I do and that they be able to make decisions and really control the direction we take. My goal is not to teach my opinion about issues like abortion or gun control. I want to focus on the process of running for office." Although these hot-button issues fuel campaigns and engage the public, as a teacher it wouldn't be appropriate for me to influence my students with my beliefs. Having them discuss the issues and debate their views as a class would provide a much more meaningful and effective lesson than having them look at the world through the tint of my sunglasses.

We started to talk about details when Kathy suddenly spoke up.

"You know, I don't think this is a very good idea. It seems that running a real election doesn't work logistically. Why don't you do a pretend election and run against Mr. Herman instead? You could each give your speeches to the students, the kids could tally their votes, and it would all be in-house. We could do it all here."

My friend Todd Herman was another sixth-grade teacher I regularly co-taught with. Kathy had also taught sixth grade before becoming an administrator, but her style had always been more "old school" than ours. I still don't believe it was wise to place her as an administrator in the school where she had been a teacher. Going from peer to evaluator was awkward and uncomfortable for everyone. She might have been more welcomed at a school where the staff hadn't been eating lunch with her and going on field trips with her classes. It's difficult to know someone and accept their flaws (we all have them), and then have them rule over you, pointing out all of yours.

When Kathy was still teaching, parents had often requested that their children be placed in my class rather than hers, which I sensed had annoyed her. How could it not? That resentment became obvious once she moved into her administrative position. Suddenly your newsletter had to be on time or your name was on a list. She frequently chewed our asses in staff meetings. And she continued to be all about the standards, something I had always adhered to, but as creatively as possible. Kathy probably figured that now that she had power, she could rein me in. Her suggestion that I stage a mock election instead of running for real was typical and absolutely unacceptable.

"That's not what the kids asked for," I said. "They asked me to prove that an average person can do this. I don't think that having a mock election with Post-it notes and a shoe box is what they're looking for here."

"I think that's really silly," Kathy insisted. "It would be so much easier if you could do it at school and then you could talk to the other grades about the election and show them your tally sheets."

Finally assistant superintendent Paul Dugan interrupted.

"Let's be clear. We cannot tell Tierney she can't run because she does have that right as a citizen."

We ended the meeting with a compromise. I would let the kids decide whether they preferred to have me run against Todd or for a seat in Congress. When I returned to the classroom, the kids were anxious to hear the outcome. I had told them that I wasn't sure this campaign would be okay with the district, and that I would do my best in the meeting to explain what we were trying to do and why we thought it was important and valuable.

"Okay, I wasn't told no. But there's also a big question. They want to know whether you all want to do it for real or whether you would prefer to stage a mock election. If we held our own election, I would run against Mr. Herman. We could pretend we were both running for governor or something."

Instead of asking the kids to discuss the option, I had them write in their journals for fifteen minutes. I didn't want anyone to be unduly influenced by the opinions of others or to try and please anyone but themselves.

My students unanimously rejected the suggestion of a mock election.

"I think we should not stop doing the campaighn,[sic]" wrote Meagan, a very bright, painfully shy girl whose mother had run off with her boyfriend, leaving the girl and her younger brother to be raised by her father. "Because it is real cool to be able to see how it feels to help the person who is running make the decision on ways that we might be able to change how your community works."

Ardean, who had been adopted by his aunt and uncle after his drug-addicted mother's death, wrote, "I really want you to run to prove that you don't have to have money too [sic] win a race that you can do it with hard work and time. I also think it would help prepare us for the world and school." I wasn't entirely surprised that Ardean, a sweet but typically rambunctious sixth grader, was already worried about dealing with the real world. Having lost his mother early, Ardean was a child who had already been called upon to handle more than his share of life's burdens.

"I definitely think you should do this!" Frank wrote. "I would love to see how a campaign works from the inside. We could help you, Ms. Cahill. This would be so awesome!" I adored Frank's parents, as well as his younger sister, who would be in my class the next year. The twelve-year-old had always been so appropriate and proper, but he was clearly loosening up. It was fun to see him get excited over the possibilities of a genuine run for office.

"I think you should do the real thing," Thomas, a struggling student with a complicated home life, stated. "You could make a difference." His plea struck me as being hopeful, an indication that he—a child I had often worried about—was reaching out with new confidence, clearly signaling that he wanted to be part of something that mattered.

The class's written vote clinched the deal, but the deal came with constraints dictated by the school district. Unless the lesson directly tied into the educational standards, the campaign could be part of the classroom curriculum only on the condition that no assignments were required, no students were obliged to participate, and no district resources such as copiers or paper were used. I would be responsible for getting through all my mandated coursework, so any extended meetings would probably have to be on my own time. We could do what we wanted after school, as long as I avoided discussing particularly sensitive and controversial issues such as abortion and gun control with my class. Finally, I had to secure permission from my students' parents, which would prove a challenge since I was a yellow-dog Democrat teaching in a very Republican neighborhood.

I sent home a letter requesting that parents attend a meeting about a project that would involve our running for office as a class, and for which I'd need their written permission if their child was to participate. Open houses and parent-teacher meetings never attract 100 percent turnouts. Many parents, especially if they're lower income, are either working or too tired to come to after-school meetings. This time the room was jam-packed, with people forced to stand at the back. Not a single parent had stayed away.

Noting the folded arms and foot-tapping, I realized they were gunning for me. I was already known as "Cay-hell" for all the homework I gave. This just made it worse. Trying to control my nerves, I made my case, explaining how the whole project had evolved, what stage we were at now, and why this was so valuable educationally. Having the students create and manage a campaign would provide a much better learning experience than simply having them read a chapter and take a test.

"I want to give the students as much power as I can," I said. "I don't think kids buy into government and social studies very much. Who cares about people in togas? Our founding fathers? Whoop-de-do! Kids don't want to know. But if they actually participate in something that's real and they're stakeholders because their decisions impact the direction we go, I think the learning is going to be phenomenal."

Despite the body language in the audience, everything seemed to be going well.

"I think this is one of those once-in-a-lifetime opportunities, and I want to honor their request," I concluded. Then I opened the floor for questions.

"So what party are you?" a dad asked.

I told them that I would rather run as an Independent and that I didn't want to get into partisan politics because I wanted the kids to focus on the process rather than on controversial issues no matter how strongly I felt about them personally. Unable to avoid the question any longer, I added, "But it's too late to change my affiliation. The class already called the Secretary of State's office, and I would have had to change parties last month. So I'll have to run as what I've always been."

"Right, and what is that?"

"Well, I'm a Democrat."

"Awww, God, I knew it!"

The note of disgust was echoed around the room. One single person in a dashiki—a mom who had been in the Peace Corps in Tanzania and was married to a professor of economics at the university—started applauding. She was thrilled. The majority of the parents, however, were not. I started to lose my nerve as angry grumbles filled the room.

Realizing that I had to sell them, I said, "Listen, this isn't about party politics. I wouldn't run as a Democrat if I had a choice, but I don't. I just want the kids to understand how to do this and the fact that it's possible. We will not get into issues. I'm not going to talk about abortion. Are you kidding me? That's not my job. That's your job. Those are your family values to convey, and those are your discussions to have over dinner. I'm not going to do that."

"Do you oppose gun control?" another parent asked.

"No, and my family hunts, by the way. But I don't even want to talk about it. And if your kid comes to me to ask what I think about gun control, I'm going to send him back to ask you what *you* think about gun control. I'm very pro-education, but I'm not going to shove my viewpoint down your kid's throat."

"I have a huge open-door policy, and you're welcome to come plant yourself in my classroom anytime," I continued.

"If you're wondering what we're doing, if you're concerned at all, please come and sit and ask the students—including your child—lots of questions. Because I think you're going to be pretty impressed with what they already know."

By the end of the evening, twenty-four of twenty-eight parents had relented and signed waivers allowing their children to participate. And as time went on, every kid would wind up being involved in one way or another, whether or not their parents had signed.

4

Which Race
Are We Running?

* * * * * * * * * * * * * * * * * * * *

"Yes!" my students yelled, jumping out of their seats. "We got her to do it!" "Wahoo!" When the celebratory eruption finally subsided, like a one-two punch the second part of my statement that morning finally registered.

"Wait. We have to manage the campaign? What does that mean? What are we going to have to do?"

"I don't know," I answered. "We're all in this together, and none of us knows anything."

I might have been ignorant about running for office, but I did know about teaching. And I knew that I wouldn't be the one figuring out what we needed to do. They would. I would simply be the one asking all the questions. That's how I teach.

The next day we started with a brainstorming session about what we would have to do to create a campaign. As usual, I started firing questions and charting the answers on the whiteboard at the front of the class. Of course, every answer triggered another question.

"What do we need to do? What kinds of things should we be thinking about?"

"We're going to have to design stuff? What kind of stuff?"

"We need signs? So where do we get them?"

"We make them? What do we make them with?"

"What's on the sign? Do we need a logo?"

"Does that mean we need an art committee?"

Committees were the way to go as far as I was concerned, since having all the kids in one group would be overwhelming. Besides, I wanted to divvy up the responsibilities and have the kids participate according to their interests, talents, and comfort levels. Not every kid likes to look up information. They needed to define their roles in the campaign, so they would feel at ease and have a more memorable experience. When you give kids control over how they learn, they buy in more.

Since I wanted the groups to evolve through the kids' own brainstorming, I didn't impose any caps. The groups could be as small—or as large—as the kids wished. The art group wound up being pretty big, though not every participant was truly talented on that front. But most had an eye for design and ideas to add, and they fed those to Robert, the art committee's clear leader because of his ability to create designs that reflected all the kids' input. At recess, kids now asked this shy boy of Korean descent to illustrate birthday cards for their moms or draw pictures of favorite animals. He had clearly come into his own.

Once we had established that an art committee was needed, we had to determine what the art committee's designs would appear on.

T-shirts were deemed a must.

"What about tote bags?" one girl asked. Someone else

wanted baseball caps. One kid even wanted to open a store-front.

"If we're going to look like a real campaign, we need to be thoughtful in our message and the way we market our-selves," I said. "Let's stick to traditional campaign materials that will be appealing to the masses."

"Oh, that makes sense," Jamie said. "We don't want ball caps, because most girls won't wear them."

"Right," agreed Robert. "And boys won't use a tote bag that looks like something their mother carries books in."

"This sounds good, since we're going to have to figure out how we're going to pay for everything," I said.

"You said we didn't need money to run for office," Heather said.

"Well, no, I didn't say we didn't need money, I said we didn't need to be millionaires."

That stopped them cold. After a few seconds, I said, "So we'll do T-shirts—most campaigns I see do T-shirts—and maybe buttons."

"Oh, yeah, buttons! We didn't think of buttons. Put that on the list!"

Undaunted by my mention of our financial constraints, the kids kept trying to expand our campaign paraphernalia.

"Sweatshirts! Yeah, we could have hoodies—the zip-up ones and the pullovers. But some people don't like hoods—we should get some without hoods, too."

I finally had to nix the sweatshirts, along with the tote bags, hats, socks, and storefront.

"Let's keep it simple, because we don't have money right now, and I don't know how much we're going to get or how we're going to pay for this. Of course, if we get really big," I conceded, "we can revisit these ideas."

I knew that wouldn't happen, but I didn't want to squash their enthusiasm.

"What other organizational groups do you think we'll need for this campaign?" I asked.

The class began to brainstorm in groups of four. Eventually Ingrid, Heather, and Frank chimed in. "We think you're probably going to need research, because you're going to have to find out stuff."

"Yep, I agree. There's a lot of information we need right now."

By the end of the day, we had also formed speechwriting, media, and finance committees. In addition, we established a managerial committee that would determine logistics such as the number of signs we would require or what we needed to do to get our name out there. I knew that by allowing the students free rein, they would undoubtedly shift from one committee to another or even participate in several at once. There would also be crossover, since the finance committee would certainly want to weigh in on plans for T-shirts being developed by the art committee. But we were on our way.

Since participation in the campaign was voluntary, I told my students that whenever they completed their classwork, they could get together to meet with their committees. The kids responsible for research got busy right away because we didn't know our rears from a hole in the ground. There were so many things to find out.

How do we run for office?

What does that mean?

When do we file?

What is filing?

Are there papers to fill out?

Where do we get those papers?

What are the deadlines?

How do we find out?

What is the cost? (How we would raise money to cover the cost fell to the finance committee.)

What should our signs look like?

Are we going to make them?

Where do we go to have them made?

How much does that cost?

The recorder for that week wrote all the questions on butcher paper or on great big Post-it notes, which were color-coded for each committee. Then we divvied up the duties.

"I want that one," said Laura, a pale, blond, straight-A student who must have gone to etiquette school to learn how to be appropriate at all times. "I want to find out where you go to file to get on the ballot."

She quickly figured out that we needed to contact the Secretary of State in Carson City for the answers. Before she called, however, we developed a script to follow so that she and the rest of the kids would know what they were talking about. And I reinforced the necessity of being polite, a point I hammered home throughout the campaign. "You say, 'Yes, ma'am,' 'Yes, sir,' and 'May I, please,' " I insisted. Then we role-played, because you can't call and sound rude and foolish, especially if you're young.

When Laura was finally ready, she sounded like a pro. "We're calling on behalf of Ms. Cahill," she said. "We're running her campaign, and we need to know, please, how much it is to file and what date she needs to do that by. What are the times she can come down? And what's involved?"

The news that we didn't need to file until May filled us all with a sense of relief. We had some breathing room. Still,

I figured that we would need to submit a statement of organization officially registering the campaign committee. We completed the paperwork, the students having decided that the committee would be called The Party of the Future— Children to Elect Tierney Cahill for U.S. Senate. Then they discovered that unless we had, or planned to raise, $10,000, we wouldn't need to file that form. I couldn't imagine that we would bring in that kind of money. It would be great if we could simply raise enough to get the buttons, T-shirts, and signs the kids had asked for. When we eventually received a check from the National Education Association (NEA) for $1,000, I nearly fell over.

Three weeks later, on my thirty-fourth birthday, my class commemorated the campaign with a big ol' birthday cake that read "Happy Birthday, Senator Cahill." Each student seemed thrilled, which made me happy since that meant that my surprise hadn't involved just a select few. They were clearly all in on it. I'd never had a class bond that quickly before. When we ate the cake at lunch recess, they went out of their way to call me Senator Cahill.

They didn't know yet that the Democratic party would be less enchanted with the notion of my running for a seat in the Senate.

Reno bills itself as the biggest little city in the world, but despite its population of more than 210,000, it's still a small town, largely run by the same families that started it. In Reno, it's all about who you know. After I applied for a teaching job, a school administrator e-mailed me back asking if I wasn't the girl who had dated Duke Rittenhouse in high school. I got the job. Seven years later, I secured my brother a job with a single phone call after his three-week search had yielded nothing.

In short, Reno is an old-boy's town, with just two degrees of separation as opposed to the typical six. Go out to run an errand and you either see someone you went to school with or meet someone who knows a kid you grew up with. This is not a town where you can behave poorly and not have everyone find out. And like most small communities, people know what you're doing whether or not you announce it. When my now-husband and I started getting serious a few years after the campaign, I regularly spent the night at his house when I didn't have the kids. One morning, my friend John Martini, who had coached my daughter, got a call from his dad.

"John, Tierney's spending the night with someone nine houses down," his father reported with a trace of alarm.

"Dad, it's okay," his son reassured him. "She's dating a friend of mine."

So I probably shouldn't have been surprised when news about our political campaign got out within a matter of days.

The week we had the parent meeting, the classroom phone rang. I picked it up expecting a secretary to tell me that Jimmy should take Bus 2 home because his mother wasn't going to pick him up, or that Sarah's mom had brought her lunch and that she should come down to the office and get it. Since instructional time is considered sacred and otherwise never disrupted, I was surprised to find that they'd put through someone whose voice I didn't recognize.

"We heard that you're thinking of running for the U.S. Senate," the caller said after identifying himself as being with the Carson City Democrats.

You're kidding, I thought to myself. *How in the world do you know that?* Later on I joked that it was like Deep Throat contacting me. The call seemed very mysterious since I had only talked to sixth graders, their parents, and some district officials. I didn't even know that there *was* a Carson City

Democrats organization, though I've since learned that most cities or counties usually have a Democratic club comprised of people active in the party.

"That's right," I answered.

"Well, you know, if your heart is set on running for the Senate, we understand and wish you good luck. And, of course, we'll support you in any way we can. But there is a guy named Ed Bernstein who is going to be running as a Democrat for that seat as well, and it wouldn't look good for the party to have someone as favorable to the voters as a public schoolteacher run against a very well-funded candidate. We'd rather spread the wealth and have you possibly run for the House instead."

He went on to tell me that Bernstein was a very successful personal-injury attorney who was pretty visible because he frequently ran TV commercials for his law practice. "And he's putting up a million of his own dollars, which certainly gives him the edge over you."

My eyes started to roll back in my head. My student's cynical pronouncement was proving prophetic, right down to the penny.

The caller went on to suggest that a run for the House would basically be an open race since Republican Jim Gibbons, a deeply entrenched conservative, had run unopposed in the 1998 election. In 1996, according to a consultant I met with, a popular Democrat named Spike Wilson had spent $685,000 running against him, but had only managed to garner approximately one third of the vote. Gibbons, a pilot who had taken part in the Operation Desert Storm invasion before serving as a state legislator, was too popular. It didn't help Wilson that our district—Congressional District 2—has forty thousand more registered Republicans than Democrats.

"We'd hate to see you and Ed Bernstein knock heads when here's this other race where no Democrats are going to run."

"I can't make that decision until I talk to my campaign committee, because this is really their deal and not mine," I responded. "Would you mind holding on for a moment? I'll ask them."

Clearly perplexed, he hesitantly agreed. "Oh, o . . . kay."

"Hey, guys, we've got to have a discussion here," I announced. "Can I get all eyes on me?"

With the caller on hold, I explained who was on the phone, why he didn't want us to run for the Senate, and what he had proposed.

"The House? Do they mean in Washington?" Rocket asked.

"Yes, it's in the Capitol building. You know, one side of the Capitol building is the Senate, the other side is the House."

"But there are more of them than there are Senators," Frank mused.

"Yes, that's true," I agreed.

"But it's still in Washington, D.C., so that's good," said Heather. "And it's still important, right?"

I explained that a bill has to go through both the House and the Senate, and that it can't go to the president to be signed into law until both have approved it.

"Well, then, okay," Ingrid and Heather concluded. "That's still pretty important."

Apologizing for keeping my caller on hold, I told him that I'd talked to my consultants and they had approved the switch. I'm sure he, like others, rolled his eyes when I said that. "Are you kidding?" they probably thought to themselves. But I did not want to downplay the kids' involvement. In this situation, they were the decision makers.

5

Fits and Starts

* *

My students needed to find their wings if this campaign was going to work. But learning to fly can be trying.

"If you win, are you going to leave us?" asked Brooks, a conscientious and academically gifted boy who was short for his age, but more than made up for that with his athletic ability. This would be the first of several almost-identical exchanges with Brooks and other students over the next six months.

"Well, I wouldn't start until the following year, so you guys will already be gone. You'll be in seventh grade by then."

"Okay, but you'll come back to Reno, won't you?" Brooks insisted.

"You won't go to Washington, D.C., forever?" Ingrid asked.

"No, no," I told them again and again. "Congressmen or -women who go there have an apartment or a house to stay in while they're in D.C., but their home is in their state."

That reassured the kids, and they got to work kicking off

our campaign. Since the class insisted that we would not be legitimate without campaign materials, creating a logo was one of the first priorities. Though we hadn't filed a single piece of formal paperwork, political vendors had already begun to send us samples of business cards and signs. We started cutting out various pictures and tacking them up on one of the class bulletin boards. The kids on the art committee—about a quarter of the class—had been struggling with what elements to use for our logo. While thumbing through one of the vendor's catalogs, however, they found a page with an image of the nation's capitol.

"Oh, that's perfect! That's the look we want."

They continued to pull bits and pieces from the various campaign documents that had been sent, eventually coming up with a number of different versions. Though they worked independently of me, I overheard them battling over the designs.

"No, that's not going to happen!" Paul argued, working hard to assert his alpha maleness. Paul's mom had married a Mormon and moved to Utah to start a new family. Blond, blue-eyed Paul had remained with his dad, a wine distributor with a huge sports memorabilia collection and a drinking problem.

"Yes, we want that!" Meagan and Ingrid retorted, determined to stand up for their ideas.

Each disagreement was put to a vote orchestrated by Robert, who ran his group with amazing maturity and seriousness of purpose, almost as if he were the Speaker of the House himself.

After three animated weeks, the team members had developed a final logo that they were ready to present. We met so that they could explain and justify their choices to me.

"Okay, obviously your last name is biggest because that's

important. The listing on the ballot is alphabetical, so you'll come before Gibbons. And people always think of him as Gibbons, even though they probably know his first name is Jim. So it's important that your last name is the biggest piece of print."

"That sounds logical and well thought out," I agreed.

They weren't done. "And 'Tierney' needs to be smaller, because that's kind of a weird name, Ms. Cahill."

"Thanks," I said with a hint of sarcasm. But they had a point. It is an unusual name. "Okay, fine. Go on."

"We need to put the year so they know when you're running. The logo should be red, white, and blue because that's patriotic and we want them to know you're patriotic." They were clearly trying their hardest to win me over. "It should have the Capitol building on there because we don't want people to think that you mean Carson City. They can look at that building—even if they're not sure what it is—and know it's in Washington."

"How many of you know what building that is?" I asked, assuming that group consensus didn't automatically imply every participant's understanding of each aspect of the project. Indeed, a number of the kids said they'd never seen the building before, even though we'd discussed it just a week earlier. I guess my whiteboard drawing didn't do the edifice justice.

"You have too seen it. Just look on the dollar bill," Robert countered. "Everybody knows what this building is," he added. "It's like the White House or the Lincoln Memorial—it's one of those famous Greek-style buildings. I'm sure it's in our textbook."

Earlier that year as part of our history unit, we had discussed how our founding fathers had modeled not only a new government, but also their choice of art and architecture, on ancient Greece and Rome. That's why so many of our public buildings in Washington, D.C., have columns and scroll-like adornments. I was downright tickled to hear Robert's explanation.

The art committee members had decided that the logo should say "Congress" to let people know what office I was running for. I guess House of Representatives got nixed because of length. They also listed my party affiliation. I've since learned that you never, ever include your party on a logo, because that can immediately turn off a percentage of the voters. If they don't know whether you're a Republican or a Democrat, you might get five minutes of their time even if they belong to a different party. But Brent, a cute little guy being raised by a single mom who worked multiple jobs, felt that "it's fair that you're honest with people and you tell them what party you are."

That was fine with me. I left the decisions to them. As long as they justified their reasons and those reasons made sense to me, we went with it. But it was hard not to giggle sometimes. They were so invested and so serious, they could have been on Madison Avenue pitching their marketing idea to Calvin Klein.

Because I wanted to empower them with every single aspect of this campaign, I tried to get my class listed on the campaign's checking account, with one student acting as official treasurer. That also fit into my agenda of trying to incorporate as many disciplines as possible into the project. What better math lesson than having the students handle a real checking account?

The bank balked. "Oh, god, no! No way! We need an adult, a tax ID number. . . ." So I had to sign up for the account under my own name and handle it myself.

I may not have been able to involve the kids directly in

the campaign's banking, but we still had class discussions about finances.

"We have this much money," I stated, once donations began to trickle in. At first the numbers weren't even in the hundreds, a far cry from the $1.3 million spent during an average campaign for a seat in the House or $9.6 million for a Senate seat.

"How much do we need for signs? How much are we getting for T-shirts? What is that going to run us?"

Although the finances were ultimately left up to me since I had to be responsible for the funds and the bank account, the kids and I always agreed on what we would spend our money on. The kids also spearheaded all the fund-raising discussions and efforts. Heather, who had proudly told me that she now got stock for her birthday and was investing in Disney, thought we should have a bake sale.

That's really precious, I thought. *Selling cupcakes to run for Congress. If it could only be so easy!*

I didn't want to be the one to say *no.* So instead of discrediting her idea, I prompted the class to analyze the suggestion. Heather launched the discussion.

"Well, let's see, if we buy ready-made cupcakes at the bakery, it will cost us about $4.99 a dozen. So if we charge a dollar a cupcake, we'll make seven dollars."

Laura chimed in. "If we make them from a boxed mix, we'll still need to get oil and eggs, and then bake them. But that means that we have to take the time to go to the store, to bake, and to sell them at recess."

Paul asked, "Wouldn't we have to submit a fund-raising form to be approved by Mrs. LaBranch?"

"Yes, we would," I confirmed.

"Well, I think the most we could charge would be fifty cents a cupcake," Meagan said.

"Is this an effective way to raise money?" I finally asked. Even Heather, who had suggested the bake sale, agreed that it wasn't. Still, I praised her for her input.

Not all the students were outwardly gung ho. There were plenty of kids who were scared to speak up even though they had ideas to contribute. They didn't get an A every week on the spelling or math test, so they felt they weren't the smartest in the class. I made sure not only to give them positive strokes, but also to watch out for the chicken hawks who too often tried to shut down their classmates.

"No, this is the best way for us to do this," the confident ones often said.

"Hold on," I always rejoined. "Let's listen to what Jacob is saying."

This verbal contest can be very gender-driven. We know girls start to become highly self-conscious during the middle school years, and that's when we begin to see a drop-off in their willingness to raise their hands and take risks with their learning. Boys are more aggressive, and tend to run over them verbally. That's one reason girls tend to be more successful, particularly with math and science, in all-girl high schools.

Though sixth graders have refined the pecking order that *The Lord of the Flies* made famous, the campaign committees helped them listen to what others said and respond with respect rather than ridicule. I insisted that phrases like *I appreciate what you said and would like to add* . . . replace knee-jerk put-downs like *You didn't say everything we could do* or *That's stupid,* which ruin the functionality of a group.

Teaching these ground rules for group work is a challenge. It's hard to make twelve-year-olds wait their turn in a conversation or to prompt a quieter kid who hasn't contributed in a while. You can watch grown-ups in meetings, and there's always someone who wants to take charge. So it was important to sit in on a lot of the committees and make sure that the timid students were allowed time to speak. More important, I wanted to teach the committees how to function that way without me there.

Building a group dynamic based on respect is hard, but it made all the difference. Instead of playing it safe and remaining on the sidelines, students felt secure enough to risk participating. As a result, even those kids who hated school and hadn't been doing well suddenly started being acknowledged for talents their classmates hadn't known they had. Robert, the talented artist, climbed from an English-as-a-Second-Language (ESL) student to class hero, which caused his self-esteem to soar. Children with specific learning disabilities also thrived in this environment. Maria, a girl whose struggles with language arts had left her extremely insecure, gained so much confidence that she became a leader in the campaign.

As a school project, the campaign was working better than I had ever imagined. But I had my own learning curve to contend with.

6

Swimming
in the Deep End

* *

I've always wanted to make a difference. A bit of an odd child at nine or ten, I tried to teach myself Russian with the help of library books. I felt sorry for the Soviet Union because of all the negative press it was getting at the time. *Maybe I could be an ambassador and help relations there and elsewhere in the world,* I thought. In the meantime, I made my stuffed cheetah, whose name was Anwar Sadat, and my lion, named Menachem Begin, sit next to each other every day after I made my bed. Side by side, they leaned against my pillows guarding my other stuffed animals and in my mind were dear friends.

The solutions seemed so simple then. They seemed less so now.

Do I even know how to be a candidate? I asked myself again and again.

The answer was a resounding *no*. I was as much a student of this campaign business as my sixth graders were.

Help came from a most unexpected quarter. The husband of a woman I knew casually, a sitting judge who had once been active in the Democratic party, had the grass-roots experience in politics that I lacked. So I put in a call and asked if he would be willing to talk to me.

"Are you a serious candidate?" he challenged right off the bat.

"Define serious," I answered. "Do I wear a Bozo nose and have an air horn? What do you mean? Do I never smile?"

"Are you really in this to win? I've got to know."

I had asked myself the same question, though never out loud. How serious was I? Did I really have the ability I needed? Because I certainly lacked the credentials. Was I really going to start a major fund-raising campaign? How would I even do that?

Somehow the judge's skepticism helped move me to an answer. It was one thing to doubt myself. Having someone else question my drive triggered every competitive instinct I had. And for a person who had gone to college on a full athletic scholarship, that was saying a lot.

"Why would anybody get in a race if they didn't want to win?" I snapped.

"Okay, fair answer," he replied. "But I want to look you in the eye and see that you're serious."

Oh my god, I don't know if I can look myself in the mirror and convince myself that I'm serious about running, I thought.

"We need to meet. But we'll have to do this very incognito."

Sitting judges are supposed to be unaffiliated and impartial. Helping me didn't fit the bill.

"All right, superspy James Bond," I quipped, unable to help myself. "Do you want me to wear sunglasses and a wig?"

"I'll meet you downtown," he said without a trace of

laughter. "You're not going to tell anybody that you're meeting with me. This has to be top secret."

"Okay," I agreed in a small voice.

We met in a tiny locally famous greasy burger joint at the back of Jim Kelly's Nugget, a dive casino on Reno's main strip that locals frequent because it has the cheapest poker tables, the cheapest craps, the best drinks in town, and, as the college students know, the best chili-cheese omelets and greasy Awful hamburgers for curing hangovers. The judge, sitting on one of the five bar stools, was wearing a tweed jacket, bolo tie with a large turquoise, and a big old hat. I could tell that he had probably been a good-looking man when he was younger. Now the years and his wild gray mustache made him look like an eccentric, fun grandpa. But he wasn't *my* fun grandpa. I was terrified. I sat on the stool next to him hoping that my choice of dress, matching jacket, and high heels, all so out of character, would make me appear like a serious candidate.

"What's your plan?" he demanded without another word of greeting. "How are you going to do this?"

Oh my god, he's grilling me, I thought.

"Jim Gibbons is a tough candidate," he continued. "He's got a lot of money, and he's got a ton of support."

The judge was so worried about "spies" that he looked forward when he spoke, so it didn't look like we were together. Though I sat to his right, he even talked over his left shoulder.

"I'm not sure how I'll win other than to be myself, be the best candidate I can be, and be as accessible as I can," I finally answered. "You know, I'm trying to do everything genuine candidates do. Yes, it is a school project, but I've made a commitment that this will be real, and to be real, you try to win, right?"

"I hope so," he answered before asking me how I was raising money.

"I'm struggling there. I don't feel very comfortable asking people for their money."

"You need to get over that. People expect it."

I knew that I should spend more time fund-raising (U.S. House candidates typically spend a third of their time doing only that) and that I should ask the big-money Reno people for campaign donations. Casino owners like John Harrah, the Caranos, or even Steve Wynn follow the money, so I needed to get some to be seen as viable. I just couldn't. I never sent out fund-raising letters. Asking for money and being denied just seemed too humiliating. I would eventually do better asking groups for money when I spoke, because those who chose not to contribute just blended into the crowd. "If you happen to feel good about this campaign and want to contribute, there's a coffee can right over there," I'd tell them.

My lack of fund-raising wasn't my only drawback.

"Do you have a consultant?" the judge asked.

"Do you mean like a hired one or do you mean my sixth graders?" I answered.

"Oh, Christ! Here we go! A real one. Have you paid for a consultant to come in and get your campaign organized?"

"No. There's no money for that," I answered. There was no money for anything at this point.

"Well, I don't know how you get to the point where you can afford one, but that would probably be one of the best uses of your money."

"Well, how much are they?" I asked.

"A good one is probably $5,000 a month."

Are you kidding? I thought to myself, choking on my iced tea.

When the judge finally realized that I simply had a group of sixth graders running everything, he shook his head, clearly stunned and a little incredulous. Then he nodded and gave me an encouraging smile.

"Listen, kid, if you're serious about this, you've got to know what you're getting into here," he said. "You gotta know how to play this game, because it's brutal. You better have some people you can go to to get information."

He started giving me names of individuals to call, as well as lists of things I needed to do and events I needed to attend. I took mad notes as he spoke, trying to figure out whether I knew the people he was mentioning as I scribbled. Every now and then he got annoyed with me, but he remained supportive, pointing me in directions I would never have known to follow. When the meeting finally ended, he shook my hand.

"Okay, I believe in you," he said. "You better not disappoint me."

"Okay, no pressure," I answered. "Great. Thanks!"

7

Party Politics

* * * * * * * * * * * * * * * * * * *

"Do we have to let anyone in the Democratic party know we're running?" Paul asked about three months into the campaign. "Wouldn't that be polite?"

We'd been so busy jump-starting the campaign that notifying the state Democrats hadn't occurred to any of us.

"How do we do that?" Heather asked.

"I don't really know," I answered. "There's a state Democratic party office. Let's try that."

We quickly found the number. I dialed and asked for the executive director.

"I'm calling to introduce myself. I'm going to be running for office," I explained when Janice Brown picked up the phone. "My class is managing my campaign. They thought you should know."

"Who said you could do that?"

"What do you mean?" I proceeded to explain how the campaign had started and that my class was running everything.

"Is this a joke? Do you think this is funny?"

"No, ma'am, this is not a prank phone call. I really am running."

"I don't think your project is amusing at all. I don't appreciate this, and I don't think the party is going to appreciate this. Have you talked to the movers and shakers in the North?"

Disgusted, I replied, "Who are they? Are they listed in the phone book under movers and shakers? You're saying I have to ask permission to run for office? I don't think so! Last time I checked, that's my right as a citizen, and just so you know, I've been a lifelong Democrat, and your attitude is very disturbing to me."

The party of inclusion was certainly not being very inclusive when it came to me. Who cared that I hadn't been approved by the party leaders? I should have the right to run for office. Was it party policy to castigate every middle-class single mom who "dared" to run?

I could have used the Dems' help—or at least their support. Running for office is a brave venture, especially if you're new. You're essentially saying, "I am willing to open myself to the press attacking me, investigating me, and sticking their nose into every crevice and hole of my life, and being subjected to criticism in the papers and more." All our veteran politicians have campaign managers and consultants who constantly spin their message to the press. I didn't have any of that, so the press would see what I was and hopefully be nice to me. But to have party people react so negatively to my campaign because I hadn't been anointed insulted me as much as it shocked me.

This woman needs to be taught a lesson on how to treat people, I thought. *I need to prove to her and to those like her that her attitude isn't just wrong, it's shortsighted.*

From then on, it was "game on" with my party, the party I

had spent a lifetime revering. The Democrats saw me as a whack job who was going to run no matter what. I'm sure I terrified them. They had no idea who the hell I was, what I was going to say, or who was handling me. When they figured out that no one was handling me, I probably seemed like a loose cannon. If they had sat down with me to talk about philosophy and platform, they would have found out that I was as die-hard a Democrat as there is. But instead of bringing me into the fold and making an effort to find out about me and my platform, they assumed that since my candidacy had started as a class project, I would embarrass them. So they wrote me off. I was not a part of the wealthy good-ol'-boy network.

Of course my students wanted to know how the conversation had gone. I hemmed and hawed about how much information to give them because I didn't want them to know how antagonistic the interaction had been. That wouldn't serve any positive purpose for the kids. I finally said, "The call has been made, and they know who we are."

Despite my party's lack of support, I began to be invited to appear at an increasing number of functions. Then I got a call from Andy Barbano, a left-wing union supporter who writes a newspaper column called "The Barbwire," requesting an interview. I've always liked him because he calls it like it is and if you're full of crap he says so in the paper. His in-your-face attitude offends a lot of people, but I think it's refreshing. We met at Java Jungle, a well-known downtown coffee shop, and sat outside overlooking the river. I must have passed muster, because after the interview he began to give me some hints, thank god, about garnering union support.

"Listen, you're going to need to go to these people and go to them early, because you'll have to prove to them that you're a serious candidate," he told me. "They're not going to give you any money unless they believe you're working hard. And you had better understand their issues. Don't walk in there if you aren't aware that this is a right-to-work state and how that undermines the unions and allows employers to fire individuals for something as petty as not wearing 'enough' makeup. Don't go in there if you don't know that the Paycheck Protection Act is a load of crap that screws the working man. You better make sure you know this stuff. Do your homework, Teacher!"

"Okay," I agreed. "Can you help me at all and explain the union's perspective on these legislative issues?"

He started expounding on each point and how it impacted middle-class families. While he came across as a little angry, he was certainly impassioned. And having grown up listening to my grandparents, I sincerely agreed with his views. Besides, my parents and grandfather had all been in unions, and now I belonged to the NEA, one of the biggest unions in the nation.

The knowledge I gained that morning enabled me to speak to the trade union members' concerns when I met them at the union hall, a one-story office building in the industrial area of neighboring Sparks, which several trade unions shared. My class came with me to a lot of their meetings, where we often saw T-shirts that read: *40-hour week? Thank the union* or *Like your weekend? Thank the union.* As I spoke, the kids moved through the blue-jeans-and-boots crowd as a unit, passing around a Folgers coffee can with "Cahill for Congress Donations" written in red marker on royal blue construction paper. Most of the contributions slipped through the slit in the can's plastic lid ranged from $1 to $5, though we also got plenty of loose change and a very occasional $20 bill. It was almost like passing the basket at mass.

The next day, the kids always counted out the nickels, dimes, and quarters of our slender take. The more substantial contributions didn't hit until the union members came to trust me. The advice, however, started flowing almost immediately.

"This doesn't have a union bug on it," a member of the painter's union announced accusatorily as he scrutinized my business card. *Bug?* I thought. *Are we talking caterpillars here?*

"What is that?" I asked.

Their big guy, Danny Thompson, Executive Secretary Treasurer of the Nevada ALF-CIO, pulled me aside.

"How did you get these done?" he asked, pointing to the cards.

"I made them at home on my computer," I said.

"Okay, so you haven't had any printed yet? When you do, you'd better go to a union shop."

The union bug, he explained, is a small trademark symbol that shows that the job has been done in a union shop. "Union members look for that bug on everything," he warned.

That had already been made quite clear.

He concluded with a caution. "If you're not supporting union businesses, you can forget about union support."

That meant not only printing our campaign literature in a union shop, but also buying union-made T-shirts when the time came. I had figured that we would get the least expensive T-shirts we could find, and have them printed at whatever cheapo depot would give me a deal. My colleague and friend Todd Herman had told me about a really good shop that had made his volleyball uniforms. I got in touch with Jake, the owner, who worked up our art so it was ready to go on shirts and buttons. Then I learned that union members never wore campaign shirts and buttons if they weren't made in a union shop. I felt horrible about having to pull my job from Jake, but I had no alternative.

The T-shirts would now cost the campaign $10 instead of $5. And since there were only two union print shops in all of Reno, one that did T-shirts and one that handled paper products, I couldn't exactly comparison shop. But I ground my teeth and grinned, figuring that these $10 T-shirts helped ensure that someone had health insurance and a decent wage, and that his or her job was controlled by fair-labor laws. This, of course, is not a concern for Republicans, since they're so anti-union anyway. That's why Democrats end up having to earn so much more!

The kids felt that we also needed stationery. Up until then, I'd been printing my letterhead using Print Shop on my computer, but it was important to them that the campaign look professional. So we ordered stationery, matching envelopes, donation envelopes, and thank-you cards (printed on the cheapest nice paper available) along with the T-shirts and buttons. They were expensive—but they were union, by god!

Explaining to my class why we'd be paying twice as much for our campaign materials wasn't easy. But at least the topic of unions had already come up.

"Why do the unions typically support Democrats?" Heather had asked a few days back. She proceeded to tell the class that her dad was a construction worker and a union member. But as a Republican, it angered him that his union dollars went to support Democrats.

"Democrats typically back union issues, so unions back Democrats," I said, trying to be as nonpartisan as possible.

"Well, my dad's upset because he likes to hunt birds and he thinks Clinton is going to make it illegal to own a gun," Heather countered.

I listened without saying a word. Personally, I sympathized with a law-abiding citizen who felt that his way of life was being threatened. I still believe that it's been a mistake for the Democrats to go after guns as aggressively as they have, especially in Nevada, with its huge sportsman population. My own father commented to me when he was dying, "Tierney, there's two things you never get rid of when I'm gone—the family guns and the truck." I still have that '57 Chevy pickup and my uncle has all of my dad's guns.

"Why do unions exist anyway?" Heather finally asked.

The history of unionizing is not something that I pretend to be an expert in. I do believe, however, that our country enjoys the quality of life we experience largely because of organized labor. The labor movement has had its controversial leaders and scandals like any other large organization. But as a member of the teachers' union, I know that the school district doesn't give us raises out of the goodness of its heart. Negotiating by our union protects our wages, health benefits, retirement, and working conditions. My mother, who worked for a large telecom company for more than twenty years, didn't have that advantage. So when they laid her and five other women off in 2005 just eighteen months before they were to retire, she was forced to create a new career for herself at the age of fifty-seven.

Of course, I wasn't about to share my personal sentiments with the kids. So I explained what unions were by using our class as an example.

"Think of our class as a group of workers, with me as your employer. If you think you should have a longer recess and I tell you *no,* that could very well be the end of the exchange. However, if you and your classmates organize and ask for a longer recess, I'm going to pay attention to the group and likely try to come up with a solution. Now I may say that we don't have time in the day for a longer recess because we have so much work to do, but with all of you pushing for more playtime, we might need to sit down and negotiate to find some middle ground so that we could both get what we wanted."

"Oh, so there's power in the number of people?" Heather asked rhetorically. She was certainly carrying this conversation.

"Well, this is a very simplistic version of this relationship, but for the most part, yes."

I asked if she knew why her dad was in the union.

"I'm not sure, but I'll ask him at dinner."

I had hoped that our campaign would trigger exactly these kinds of interactions—with luck her father would feel the same way. Chances were good that I'd find out firsthand at a union meeting, since I was becoming a regular.

About once a week I'd show up at a union event with my new union-label campaign materials in hand. Getting the AFL-CIO on your side—which encompasses several subsidiary trade unions, including the carpenters, plumbers, ironworkers, and welders—is huge. So there was a lot at stake. Still, I was too scared the first time to do anything more than just sit in the back and watch their meeting. I wanted to see what it was like before jumping in. You would have thought these guys—a gruff lot dressed in blue jeans, work boots, and plaid shirts—had just gotten off work. When they briefly introduced me, I waved, thanked them for letting me be there, and asked if I could come again.

By the next visit, I was ready to speak. Since Barbano had coached me on union issues, by that point I knew them backward, forward, upward, and downward. I certainly hadn't needed prompting on the importance of unions, which I felt were instrumental in keeping the working class, myself included, above water.

My first speech was less than brilliant. I was so terrified when I stepped up to the podium that I knew I was going to throw up. I didn't mind talking to thirty kids and being funny as I taught, but the idea of addressing a bunch of adults who were very aware, involved, and up on the issues made me nauseous. I managed not to hurl, but that was about the only thing working in my favor. I went on and on about how my dad was a union guy, and how my mom worked, and how my stepdad was in a union shop and was a union leader. Unfortunately, instead of bonding with them, I was boring them.

Desperate to grab their attention, I concluded on a personal note.

"I'm not sure I understood what all this meant in terms of politics until my son Kelton was a kindergartener and it was button day," I told them. "Before school he asked, 'Can I get a button out of your drawer, Mommy?' I had collected buttons and had a box full of them. I didn't think much about it as I rushed to get all three children ready. At the end of the school day, he came down to my classroom wearing the button he had selected, one of my dad's from the 1970s, that said 'Ronald Reagan is a Union-Busting S.O.B.' I gasped and said, 'Oh dear god, did you wear that to class today?' 'Yeah, you said I could grab a button, Mommy.' Almost choking, I said, 'Oh boy, what did your teacher have to say?' He answered, 'Well, she said it was very interesting.' "

The story made them laugh.

"At least you're raising your son right," one of the guys quipped. Similar comments flew around the room. Suddenly they liked me.

I quickly realized that being myself was the key to connecting with my audience. That was helpful, since I wouldn't have known how to do anything else.

"I wonder if Jim Gibbons knows how much milk is selling for right now, because milk is killing me," I would later repeat at event after event, invoking the Republican incumbent even though I was technically running against other Democratic contenders in this primary race. Milk prices had climbed to the outrageous price of $2.50 a gallon, which meant that I had to worry about how many gallons my three children were going to drink each week. "I wonder if he even does the shopping. Does he know which store has the sale this week? Do you think he waits for the Sunday paper so he can clip coupons before he goes grocery shopping?"

Working-class people always laughed. They got it. "You're a real person," I heard at the end of most of my talks. Clearly that was something new and refreshing when it came to political figures.

8

Holiday Madness

★ ★ ★ ★ ★ ★ ★ ★ ★ ★ ★ ★ ★ ★ ★ ★ ★ ★ ★

The campaign briefly took a backseat as I worried about Christmas, a holiday I hated because every year I could ill afford presents or even a tree. The holiday season always reminded me of how little we had and how unfair I felt that was to my children. They were awesome little kids, and I felt so guilty that no matter how hard I worked, there was never enough. It wasn't like I was what Republicans love to degrade—a welfare mother milking the system. I worked really hard, but we weren't making it. Frustrated and ashamed, I'd silently visit my own demons and wonder what I had done to deserve this.

People don't think of teachers as underpaid, but my own children qualified for free and reduced lunches, which meant that we fell below the poverty line. How sad is that? Socioeconomically, our family ranked in the bottom twenty-fifth percentile even though I was a college-educated, award-winning teacher. The only way to make decent money within the school system would have been to leave the classroom and go into administration. That wouldn't have worked even if I had wanted to do that, which I didn't. There's a reason that most administrators are male, even though men comprise a very small percentage of the teaching population. Administrator hours are very long. My principal arrives at school by 6:30 or 7:00 in the morning and she doesn't leave until 5:30 or 6:00 at night. Even then, she often has to run back for a night basketball or football game that lasts until 10 or 11 p.m. That's almost every day. Whenever there's an after-school function—and at a high school there are a zillion—an administrator always has to be there. So the demands on an administrator's time are huge, and those demands limit the playing field. If you are a woman with a family, good luck, because it's probably not going to happen. Women who go into administration usually do not have children or their children are grown.

Just to survive, I had to supplement my inadequate teacher's income with unreliable tips from my waitressing job and the occasional real estate commission. When you're at that financial level, things go in cycles. You keep your head above water for a while, and then something unexpected happens. Your car breaks down or your kid gets sick, and suddenly you are out of balance again because there isn't any extra to absorb the unanticipated expense. Those little bumps send everything flying. Of course, the holidays are always the worst. That's money that's not there. Christmas brought to light the shortfall I tried so hard to hide. I couldn't stand that time of year.

On the last day before the two-week break, I didn't even want to leave my classroom, so I stayed well past the dinner hour. I couldn't face going home and confronting the reality of another Christmas and disappointing my three children yet again. Derrick, my boyfriend, did little to help. Though he owned multiple homes, he'd buy the kids a calendar from the dollar store. One year he bought a pine tree that was half dead and falling over, with the intention of planting it in the yard once the holiday was over. How embarrassing for the kids to have to thank him for that pathetic Charlie Brown Christmas tree. When he did do something nice, there was always a price to pay. I learned not to take anything from him if I could help it, because he would always use it against me later.

When I finally walked out to the parking lot that night, after delaying as long as possible, my car was the only one left. So I knew it had to be mine, even though a large, freshly cut Christmas tree that I certainly hadn't purchased lay tied to its roof.

Who could have done that? I wondered.

Then I discovered that the anonymous donor had also filled my backseat with groceries, a box of ornaments, and wrapped presents for the kids. When I opened the trunk to deposit my bookbag, I found even more bounty.

My sense of immense relief and gratitude was rivaled only by terrible embarrassment that my need for help had been noticed by someone.

Is it that obvious that we aren't making it? I wondered. *I thought I did a better job of hiding our struggles.*

I recalled a prior Christmas when a family of strangers had shown up at our house.

"Hi, are you Tierney?" they asked. "We have some things for you."

They walked in the house with bags of groceries and proceeded to fill my kitchen countertop with food and presents. You could tell someone had told them that I was a single mom with kids the same ages as theirs.

"Oh! We are so happy to meet you!" they said.

I am the scum of the earth right now, I thought. *Are you kidding?*

I had experienced the same feeling once before during our school's Thanksgiving food and clothing drive, run by Evelyn Mount, an eightyish-year-old black grandmother from the lower socioeconomic part of town. Like many black matriarchs, she means business when she sets her mind to something. So when Penny LaBranch first became the principal at Rita Cannan Elementary twenty years ago, Mrs. Mount came up to the school demanding to know who her families were going to be for Thanksgiving and why she hadn't been given that information yet. Penny wasn't exactly sure what she was referring to. Mrs. Mount didn't have a lot of time to get this new principal up to speed, so she sternly told Penny that she needed a list of any child that Penny suspected of being in need, how many family members they had, and their address. "Get hopping," she concluded. "There's no time to waste."

Penny held on to the tradition when in 1994 she opened Sarah Winnemucca as a new school. Teachers were expected to get on board with this and help any way they could. That could mean donating money to Mrs. Mount, purchasing whatever she might require (and she'd tell you, "I need twenty more turkeys in the next hour!"), donating used coats, or contributing time at Mrs. Mount's garage, where local contractors had built floor-to-ceiling shelving to hold all the canned goods.

Todd and I held a food-drive competition to see which class could donate the most canned goods. Though the entire school was participating in the drive, ours was a drive on steroids. My students repeatedly staked out the nearby shopping center to ask for donations. Then they had me hit the Grocery Outlet across town, which they'd found an ad for in the paper. Since the canned goods sold there were off brands or dented, I could buy ten cans for a dollar. Every morning we tallied up our numbers to see which class was ahead.

The winning class was to buy the other class pizza. Though my kids ended up ahead, everyone really won. So Todd and I bought all of our kids pizza, and we celebrated during the half hour it took to load the truck that Penny then drove over to Mrs. Mount's house.

That Wednesday night, I went to Mrs. Mount's to help fill grocery bags with food. She called everyone working the assembly line "sweetheart" or "honey," and made him or her feel as if they were family and she'd known them forever. Then she asked me to deliver food to a number of families living in a motel, including an elderly couple raising their three young grandchildren, who had been taken away from their drug-addicted mother. When I handed Grandma three bags of groceries and a turkey, she began to cry. "I have more for you," I said, going back to the car for the winter coats Mrs. Mount had given me for the children. Upon my return, the woman told me through her tears that her husband had recently suffered a stroke and was no longer able to work. "I'm working two jobs trying to take care of us all, but my husband is weak, and I worry about leaving the three little ones with him when I'm at work."

I left feeling grateful for what I had, but tremendously discouraged about the plight of this poor family. As I finished the night with Mrs. Mount and bid her good-bye, she made me put a basket of food in my car to take home. Unbeknownst to me, Penny had listed mine as being a family in need. I cried the whole way home.

Despite what people say, there's no dignity in being poor. It's a totally humiliating experience that I don't know that people are ever better for. I had tried so hard to pretend that we were making things work. Apparently I wasn't the best actress. The fact that someone had seen through the facade was even more demoralizing than the state of our finances. And now it had happened again.

Whoever had filled my car and topped it with a Christmas tree was clearly trying to protect my dignity by remaining anonymous. Unable to do anything but accept the gift, I sat in my car and sobbed for half an hour, caught in a tornado of thankfulness, mortification, and anger.

Over the unexpectedly plentiful holiday, I kept wondering about the identity of our benefactor. I knew the school janitor could tell me. That last afternoon before the break, he had come to my room to ask for my car keys.

"I need to plow the teachers' driveway, so I'll have to move your car," he said.

His request had surprised me, but I gave him my keys and didn't think any more about it. Now I realized that he had obviously been in on the plot. I also realized that he had surely been sworn to secrecy. Not wanting to put him in an awkward position, I never asked him about the incident. Years later, I found out that my best friend, Stacey Melcher, a fourth-grade teacher, and her firefighter husband, Todd, had played Santa that year. They were also responsible for the sporadic $50 and $100 gift certificates to Winco Foods (where we could buy cheap groceries in bulk) that would show up in my school mailbox. The certificates were always signed "The Angels."

The unknown angels pulled me through Christmas emotionally as well as financially, and life began to normalize until campaign muck disrupted any sense of serenity. We had just walked through the front door one night when the phone rang.

"It's late. Go get ready for bed," I told the kids as I headed to answer the call. When I picked up, an angry male voice barked, "Do you have any idea what you're doing? You're embarrassing this party. Get out now." His message didn't disturb me. I'd heard it before. A month prior, a caller—perhaps the same one—had accused me of "making a joke out of this race and the party." *Wow, that was really mean,* I'd thought. Then I'd dismissed the event from my mind. But the tone of voice on this call frightened me.

"Who is this?" I asked. My voice must have sounded afraid.

"What's wrong, Mommy? Who was that?" Kelton asked when I hung up.

I tried to check my voice and replied, "I don't know. Probably a wrong number." Standing still in the narrow, dark hallway, I stared at the phone cabinet that was built into the wall, wishing I had a phone with caller ID, then forced myself to think about getting the kids settled down. I'd try to organize this incident in my mind later. If I said anything more about it now, I would scare the children.

After I got the kids to bed, I plopped down on my tapestry couch in the living room and tried to dismiss the call from my mind. I never liked being at home with the kids alone at night. I never slept well; I heard every little noise and often worried about what could happen if anyone tried to break in. Instead of letting my fears take over the night, I turned on the TV to have noise in the room with me as I went around and locked all the doors and windows. Then I went to work reading my e-mail, and trying to get ready for the next day by checking my calendar and making lunches. The house was

very cold, but the oil furnace started to kick on in the unfin-
ished cement basement where the boys had their room. I felt
terrible that they had to stay in the dark and dingy basement
with its exposed beams that seemed to constantly grow cob-
webs, but in a 900-square-foot house, that was the only option. Kennedy's room was just too small for all three of them.
I looked in on the kids before finally heading to bed, unable
to dispel a sense of trepidation.

*What had I done to make someone so upset with me? Why
was there so much anger? Was someone upset because I'd
proved to be a better candidate than he anticipated? Or was it
someone within the Democratic party who was still pissed off
that I was running at all?*

I was well aware that you meet some freaks of nature on
the campaign trail—people who want to be buddy-buddy
with you . . . or not. Individuals who are part of the crowd
suddenly feel like they have the right to say anything they
want to you. When you're pregnant, total strangers think
they have the right to touch your tummy. "I don't even know
you," you want to say. "Why are your hands on me?" When
this same sense of entitlement is exhibited toward you as a
candidate, it's even more disquieting because no matter how
bizarre people get, you must play nice and not offend anybody. But there's no guarantee that *they're* going to play nice
with *you,* as the guy on the phone had clearly demonstrated.

Have I inadvertently offended someone? I asked myself.
*Who is this? He's clearly on a high horse. But does his lack of
boundaries mean he's unbalanced?*

Up until now, I had felt tried by the campaign, but never
frightened. But this really gave me pause.

Why am I doing this? I asked myself. *What if someone
came to my house and wanted to hurt us? It's not simply me
here.*

For the first time, I felt afraid for my children. Though I didn't sleep well that night, by the next morning I had determined not to let my fears run my campaign and to face head-on the challenges that were bound to keep cropping up.

9

Everyone Has
an Agenda

★ ★ ★ ★ ★ ★ ★ ★ ★ ★ ★ ★ ★ ★ ★ ★ ★ ★ ★

"I'm going to run against you," announced Diane Hart, a feminist Democrat from Las Vegas who was loaded with money. "I think I'm a better candidate, and I'll have a better chance of unseating Gibbons than you."

I had just returned home after an unexpected weeklong trip. News that my little brother had collided with a tree at 3 a.m. and was in critical condition had sent me racing to Sacramento. I went by the grace of my ex-husband, who took our kids, and by my fellow teachers. Since teachers are only allowed one personal day per year, four of my colleagues claimed sequential personal days and then sent the substitute down to my classroom so that I could stay by my brother's bedside in the intensive care unit. This allowed my parents to go home at night and get some sleep, and ensured that my brother was never alone. Though he had flat-lined immediately after the accident and had broken ribs (along with a host of other bones) that had punctured his lung, thankfully he survived.

"Okay, but I'm not quitting," I responded to the woman on the phone. "I made a promise."

I suddenly realized that if I didn't own this campaign and really want it deep down, I could very easily make it go away. It was up to me. And while I had believed in the project, our ideals, and our goals from the start, having to fight for what we were doing cemented my conviction.

"Well then, tell me why you're running."

The more Hart heard about the class project, the more she questioned my seriousness and my ability to run a good race.

"Jim Gibbons needs to be beaten. If you're not prepared to do that, I'm going to jump in this race."

"Hmm," I answered.

"I'd like to meet with you so we can discuss this further and then decide which one of us is going to run."

I am running no matter what, so you're not going to talk me out of that, I thought. *But okay, I'll meet with you.*

I wondered about her agenda. During a campaign, everyone involved has one, and I have been down some strange roads thanks to other people's agendas.

"I got a question for you," the father of one of the girls to whom I was giving softball pitching lessons announced one afternoon during my subsequent brief exploratory campaign in 2004. "What do you think about prostitution?"

Are we talking about me and my daughter here or what? I thought. *That's such a weird question, especially coming from a retired IRS auditor who now conducts private financial investigations for companies.*

"You mean how do I feel about prostitution being legalized here in our state?" I said once I collected myself. Out of Nevada's seventeen counties, ten allow prostitution and two tolerate it.

"Yeah, yeah, exactly, that's what I mean. How do you feel about that?"

"I don't care. I figure if it's regulated, the gals get tested and the psychos have a place to go rather than raping someone on the street. So I guess I'm fine with it, though I don't want my daughter to be one, and I'm sure not doing that to make extra money."

"Okay, okay. I needed to make sure because Dennis Hof would like to meet with you," he said, explaining that Hof was the owner of the Moonlite Bunny Ranch, a brothel located four miles east of nearby Carson City.

"Is that the show on HBO?" I asked.

I didn't have HBO, but I had heard about their adult series, which portrayed the mini-dramas that happen within the Bunny Ranch.

"Yeah, yeah, the same guy."

"Oh my god, why does he want to meet me?"

"Well, because you're a candidate and you're pro-education."

I was stunned. Unable to think of a retort, I agreed to meet Hof as long as I didn't have to go to the whorehouse.

"Actually, he'd like to have you to his home."

"Eew!" I exclaimed, my nerves kicking in.

Is this like the Mafia? I thought. *Who are these people? What are they like? Are there hookers running all over the house?*

Eventually, curiosity prompted me to go. I had to find out what he wanted and why he wanted to talk to me.

Hof's ranch sits on the southwest side of Washoe Valley, a very upscale rural neighborhood outside Reno with a shallow lake on one side and the high-peaked, densely forested, snow-topped Slide Mountain on the other. I drove past a number of prosperous ranches with immaculate barns, indoor riding facilities, water features, and rolling grassy landscapes before arriving at Hof's gated entrance. Once I'd been buzzed in, I proceeded down the long driveway lined with large pine trees and lush bushes, and parked in front of a white ranch house with a narrow, bare porch that seemed to lack a woman's touch.

A bodyguard met me at the door and escorted me in. That made me even more nervous. I had worn a dress suit and schoolteacher pumps in an effort to look as matronly as possible, a move that seemed downright brilliant when I realized that Hof's house was filled with men, including his attorney, his tax guy, his PR guy, his private chef, his bodyguard, and the father I knew who had set up the meeting. As we passed the kitchen, I looked in.

"That's Ron Jeremy!" I exclaimed.

I had recently seen *Porn Star,* a documentary about a special-education teacher who had traded education for the porn industry. My girlfriends had urged me to go, saying that it was hysterical.

"Any gal who knows about Ron Jeremy is definitely getting my money," Hof announced, laughing. I later found out that Jeremy is one of Hof's closest friends.

I could feel a bright red flush spreading across my face.

"Oh, dear god! No! It's not like I'm a big porno fan or know porn stars! I just happened to see this movie . . ."

"Oh, no, no, no," he interrupted. "You've already won my money, but we'll talk more about that soon."

Hof led me into what he called his "war room," where black leather chairs had been set up in a circle so you could see everybody and Persian rugs adorned hardwood floors. Explicit crotch shots of a very platinum blonde, framed and matted, adorned the walls of this clearly masculine retreat.

"Oh, good lord!" I gasped.

"Oh, I'm very sorry, does that offend you?"

"Well, no," I answered. "I have a vagina. I guess I'm just not used to such public display."

"I'm so sorry. She was a girlfriend of mine," he explained. "You understand?"

Oh, Jesus! You've hung your girlfriend there for the world to see? I thought. *How nice of you.*

"So you're probably wondering why I wanted to meet with you," Hof said.

Right! I have no idea why you'd want to meet with me.

"Well, I love that you're pro-education."

"Thank you, I think."

"I love that you're pro-education because I'm also pro-education."

"O . . . kay," I said, still not understanding what he was driving at. "Could you explain your thinking to me? Because I'm not following you. Are you saying you want more money for education?"

"Oh, absolutely," he said.

"Really? Okay, so if that meant raising taxes you would be okay with that?"

"Oh, absolutely. In fact, I have a good story for you. You know who Joe Conforte is?"

I knew that Conforte had run the Mustang Ranch until the IRS seized it in 1990 because of tax evasion. Oddly, the federal government actually ran the brothel, but proved less successful than Conforte. The Ranch was padlocked (for the first time) within a few months. To recover some of its tax debt, the IRS auctioned off the brothel's contents, including its bidets, and sold it in 1991 to what turned out to be one of Conforte's shell companies. He didn't hold on to it for long, however, since he was forced to flee to Brazil when the IRS busted him for racketeering and money laundering a few years later. Eventually, the brothel's newest owner (the Federal Bureau of Land Management) sold the Mustang Ranch on eBay to now-prominent brothel owner Lance Gilman for $145,100.

I also knew that fifty years prior, Conforte had opened an illegal brothel some forty miles outside of Reno and promptly tangled with then–District Attorney of Washoe County Bill Raggio, now the Nevada Senate Majority Leader. In an effort to discredit Raggio, Conforte tried to set him up with the underage sister of a prostitute. That cost Conforte twenty-two months behind bars and his Triangle River Ranch Brothel, since Raggio torched it. Conforte complained that "the order said abate the nuisance, not burn it." Raggio replied simply, "I abated the nuisance."

Hof confirmed my facts and then launched into his story. "Well, Joe went down to testify before the state legislature that they should raise taxes from 4.279 to 5 percent because the girls could figure out those numbers a lot more easily in their heads." I laughed, imagining the state legislators' reaction to the idea of raising taxes so that prostitutes could calculate them more readily.

"I have a different thought on education," Hof said. "I think it's important for a society to be well educated because the better educated they are, the more money they make, don't you agree?"

"Well, usually, there are more opportunities for people and they are able to have more choices in life and that can certainly lead to making a better living, I suppose."

"I want to see as many people graduate from high school

and college and all of that because I figure the more money they make, the more expendable income they have," Hof affirmed. "And the higher the income, the more creative they get when it comes to how they spend their money."

I finally started to understand. Hof figured that higher education supports his industry because those educated men can afford his services. So promoting education was a high priority for him.

In this campaign, my potential opponent Diane Hart's agenda involved doing everything in her power to get Jim Gibbons out of office for one main reason. He was pro-life and she was pro-choice. With her money and connections, she figured she had a much better chance of beating him than I. She was in good with the Red Rock Democratic Club in North Las Vegas's Summerlin area—a new neighborhood comprised of upper-end, gated communities—and could no doubt count on its financial support. I was disappointed about her prospective candidacy, since she would be tough to beat. Still, she was obviously on the fence about running, since she wanted to talk to me in person.

We met at the Reno airport bar minutes after her plane from Las Vegas landed. Like the judge, she said she needed to look me in the eye before making up her mind about me. I wondered why they both felt that they could only get a sense of my commitment and conviction in person. Maybe they were used to shysters who are good salesmen on the phone.

Over iced tea, I reiterated that I was in this race to stay whether or not she ran. Hart, a very assertive, articulate, well-to-do woman who reminded me a bit of Hillary Clinton, didn't waste any time on banter.

"Where do you stand on abortion?"

"Even though I grew up Irish-Catholic, abortion has never been a religious issue for me," I explained. "I'm totally pro-choice with one exception. I believe in parent notification. I can't even give Tylenol to a kid who has a headache in my classroom. But I can take her to get an abortion without her parent's consent? I have a problem with that. Who's going to monitor that minor mentally, emotionally, and physically after such a procedure? How do you not involve a parent in that?" I added that though I'm pro-choice and in all other regards don't think the government should be involved in legislating this issue, I wouldn't call myself a cheerleader for abortion. I think any unwanted pregnancy is a tragedy no matter what decision the woman makes, since it will impact her for life. This tragedy is compounded when a minor becomes pregnant. But she—and her parents—must live with her choice, one that a parent needs to be allowed to help her make.

Though we disagreed about parental notification, I obviously believed in a woman's right to choose. Hart started to feel me out on the rest of the Democratic platform, including taxes. She disapproved of tax cuts for the rich. They had more, she felt, so they should pay more. We certainly had no argument there.

The more she heard about my beliefs and my background, the more she liked me. I think she thought, "Okay, well, if you are serious and are going to work hard, then go for it, but you are going to need a lot of help." So she invited me to come down to Vegas to start getting connected and getting my name out there. Forty-five minutes to an hour after landing in Reno, she got back on a plane and went right back home, never having set foot out of the airport.

A few weeks later at Hart's invitation and expense, I flew to Vegas—a community decidedly more Democratic than

Reno—to woo the local constituency. I stayed at her beautiful home with cats everywhere and a pool. I am superallergic
to cats, so that made me uncomfortable. But the cats were
easier to deal with than the lack of friendliness. I knew that
Hart wasn't exactly cuddly, but I still hadn't expected such a
cold, businesslike attitude. So I was eager to head to the Red
Rock Democratic Club's Saturday picnic and do what I'd
come for.

Shelley Berkley, a Democratic Congresswoman from
District 1, which is essentially made up of downtown Vegas,
had been invited to speak at the public park event. The
ballsy, assertive politician was great—lots of fun and highly
organized. I had never seen a candidate in action like that.
Her volunteers and staffers, all wearing "Berkley Brigade"
T-shirts, handed out so many buttons and other campaign
paraphernalia that everybody there was layered in her good-
ies. She delivered her fifteen-minute speech to enthusiastic
acclaim, collected some checks, and moved on to her next
event.

Her operation concerned me as much as it interested me.
I certainly didn't have the kind of money that buys paid
campaign people to be on their cell phones, saying, "Okay,
Tierney will be here in fifteen minutes. Make sure this is all
ready." I didn't have foot soldiers, other than little sixth
graders, to set things up. And if I *did* have my volunteers
with me, it was because a mom had offered to drive them.
That was clearly not a factor for most politicians. On the
other hand, they didn't have the honesty and sincere hearts
of my sixth-grade clan. There was something so incredibly
charming about them on the campaign trail. Campaign
workers, many of whom are volunteers, are somewhat excited about their candidates to be sure, but you never know
their motives. Some of the most deeply entrenched hope for

positions on the candidate's office staff should the election propel their candidate into (or back into) office. But when children hand you a button and ask you to please vote and learn about the candidates, it's hard not to follow up with questions about what they're doing.

Holding people's attention was tougher when I was on my own. During the two to three hours I spent with the Red Rock Democratic Club, I probably talked to forty different people. The reception was mildly warm at best. They thought Berkley was great, but they had no idea who I was and seemed annoyed by what they perceived as my little class project. Hart introduced me to a small group that I talked to for ten to fifteen minutes before being moved to another group of people. I also met another candidate, Tom Collins, running for the state legislature. I had a hard time not giggling at his name, and wondered what kind of smart-alec questions he had to field, what with having the name of a cocktail. Of course, in Nevada that was probably a plus.

Each time I had an opportunity to gain the attention of a group of the attendees, I explained how I had gotten into this situation, why I loved the idea of politics, and that I was willing to work hard as a candidate and do what I needed to do to represent my party well.

"I've always thought that my job as a person is to be well informed, to be well read, and to vote. As a teacher, I have the honor of being a public servant," I told them. "Prompted by my students, I now want to move beyond that and be a public servant to more people at a higher level.

"I wish public service was respected and honored like it used to be," I added. "Being a public servant has a different connotation than it once did. Now it's perceived as self-service or corporate service. But working on behalf of the people should be a noble thing. I am willing to do that."

Out of respect for my students and their parents, I tried to stay away from controversial issues. Since education is truly important to me, I talked about making sure that the schools were well funded. Nevada ranks forty-sixth nationally when it comes to funding public schools. We spend about $6,500 a year per student. Compare that to Connecticut, where they spend over $12,000 per student.

They threw some test questions at me, things like "What do you think about us cutting funding for birth control in Africa?," "What should we do about immigration?," and "What's your position on embryonic stem cell research?" If you are a party-line Dem, which I was, you know the answers to all of those. So that wasn't hard to manage.

The challenge lay in what was left unsaid. Having been told that this was a picnic, I had worn a pair of khakis, a sweater vest, jacket, low heels, and my Target costume jewelry. Berkley, on the other hand, had worn pearls with her campaign T-shirt. She had a perfect haircut and flawless makeup, and looked like she fit in. Upper-class people have badges—women carry Coach or Prada purses and wear Ray-Ban sunglasses. When you have none of those adornments, it's very evident that you are not in that club. Nobody has to say anything; it's an immediate visual.

I could tell that my shoes were being checked out. My earrings were being checked out. My hands were being checked out, and the fact that I didn't have a French manicure was being judged. I couldn't afford a manicure or pedicure. If I was lucky enough to have a half-dead bottle of fingernail polish that hadn't completely dried up in the bathroom cabinet, maybe I'd paint my toenails. Otherwise, forget it.

I found the ostentatious wealth and obvious scrutiny of my clothes and jewelry troubling. "Are you really one of us?"

they seemed to be asking. I had a hard time reconciling their unspoken judgments and condescending smiles with the kind of Democrats I was used to—union people interested in finding someone to fight for their interests. These folks seemed to be more interested in access and visibility, and they were clearly not banking on me to provide that. I wanted to ask this group, "Are you people sure you're in my party?"

That question was becoming the refrain of my candidacy.

Still, I didn't return home empty-handed. Though none of the Red Rock women offered to help my campaign with time or money, Hart's mother, whom I hadn't met, donated $1,000. Her daughter had obviously directed her to write a check. That first donation was later followed by another $1,000 each from Hart and her mother.

As far as the kids were concerned, the thousand dollars I brought back from Vegas could have been a million. They were thrilled that the contribution, our first significant one, would help us become legitimate. Up until now, when people asked whether we had a campaign sign, we'd answer, "Well, not yet." And they immediately concluded that we were not for real. We could now purchase basic campaign necessities that would prove invaluable in getting people to take us seriously.

10

The Education of Candidate Cahill

★ ★

I don't know how to half-ass anything, because it haunts me to do a bad job. I have a very competitive nature. Coming from a family of professional athletes (my uncles and my grandfather all played pro baseball), I, too, wanted to be the best in whatever arena I competed in. The best athlete. The best teacher. The best candidate. Even Kelton, Kennedy, and O'Keeffe will tell you that I do whatever it takes to win . . . or at least to compete with excellence. As a high school senior, I was already an admitted perfectionist. I didn't go to my prom because I had an appointment to see a college coach a day or two later. Wanting to make sure my drop ball worked, I trained with my pitching coach that night. Even while writing this book, my husband, Brandon, can't stand that I will edge the yard and then go back over it two or three times, because I haven't gotten it exactly right.

"You're the only one who sees that," he reminds me each time.

"I know that!" I answer. "And it bugs me!"

The more I learned how to be a candidate, the more my

candidacy evolved, and with more responsibility came more expectations and more demands. Much of the time my Pollyanna side would kick in and I would figure that everything was going to work out fine. *I am doing what I am supposed to be doing and doing a pretty good job considering the circumstances,* I'd tell myself. As long as I made this a proud, honorable, and dignified experience for the children, I felt like I was adhering to my own ethical standards.

The more meetings I went to, however, the more I realized that I *had* to understand the concerns of my constituency. The Internet was somewhat helpful, but local issues required that I read the local paper. For the first time, I got a subscription to the *Reno Gazette-Journal* and started setting my alarm forty-five minutes earlier than usual so that I would have time to go through it. I had always purchased the paper on the weekends, but since my drive to work was about a half hour, during the week I usually got my news from National Public Radio (NPR). That wouldn't do any longer. I'd have to make sure I read everything every day.

Though I had been operating on pure instinct until now, I also realized that I needed professional advice. At the judge's suggestion, I phoned the office of State Attorney General Frankie Sue Del Papa, a dynamo and one of the most powerful women in the state during my campaign. Tremendously popular with the public, she was outspoken and bright, and seemed a true Nevadan. She could even sing our state song, "Home Means Nevada," word for word. I was nervous about approaching her, but I figured that since the judge had told me to ask her for guidance, some secret Democratic chick knowledge would be passed on to me during our meeting.

When I got to her office at the end of the day, Del Papa was still in a meeting with staff members. By the time she emerged at 5:30 p.m., she said, "I'm sorry I don't have much time for you. I have a fund-raiser I need to get to. If you'd like to walk me to my car, we can talk on the way." I had hoped that she'd fill my brain with tremendous knowledge and wisdom. Instead, she seemed confused about what I wanted of her. It sounds simple, but I didn't know how to tell her that I was looking for her support, help, and advice. I admired her so much that I felt way out of my league. When we reached her car, she wished me good luck in my campaign. I walked away feeling like the political neophyte that I was. I would have been stunned and most humbled to know that in 2001, I would be honored by the attorney general's office as a Women's Role Model.

I had better luck with Debbie Smith, a former Nevada state legislator and president of the PTA for the state of Nevada who was running to regain the seat she'd lost when realignment changed her precinct. Pro-schools and pro-unions, she was warm and generous with her advice.

"You probably need to meet with the Progressive Leadership Alliance of Nevada," she told me. "They do candidate trainings for just $100."

The Progressive Leadership Alliance of Nevada (PLAN) is a nonprofit organization that reminds me of Common Cause. Very grassroots and of the people, it supports workers' rights and is always ratting out in the press legislators who support positions that aren't good for families or Nevadans. In an effort to get progressives elected, PLAN holds trainings for candidates running for anything from city council to national office, and educates them about how to organize a campaign.

During the training, a consultant from Oregon showed us how to evaluate the number of voters you needed to reach to get elected and therefore how many you had to reach each week. He made us structure all this in our brain and on paper so that it was realistic.

"How are you going to reach those voters and how much is it going to cost?" he asked. "If you have to raise this much money, how many people does that mean you must call a day?"

Though I was the only national candidate there, a lot of the participants had a whole lot more knowledge and experience than I did, which really helped. During roundtables, they shared what had worked for them along with suggestions about who to talk to. I took notes, asked lots of questions, and felt thankful that I had a safe place to get the training I so desperately needed.

Though the campaign was proving more time-consuming than I had ever anticipated, as doors opened, I felt compelled to walk through. *That's what a real candidate would do,* I told myself each time. I knew that when the campaign was over, I didn't want to have a single regret that if I had only shown up for one more event, it would have made a difference. So I kept pace with my increasingly demanding campaign schedule, despite the fact that I was more and more aware of not being included in official party functions that Democrats from other campaigns were attending.

I was no longer surprised that I was being shunned on the state and national levels. But I *had* expected to be acknowledged and included at the local level. In hindsight, I'm sure that the Washoe County Democrats' executive director, Shane Piccinini, simply announced that "There's this crazy teacher with a wild hair up her ass who thinks she can run for Congress. We're not wasting any resources on her. She wants to make it a class project? Fine. But we have real candidates to worry about. Be polite, but we're not helping her."

Thankfully, not all Nevada Democrats in the know felt that way. The judge continued to give me his thoughts about whom I might approach for support. Kendall Stagg, a super-brilliant ball of fire in his mid to late twenties who was running for the state assembly, also came to my rescue. Stagg, whose tremendous vocabulary was rivaled only by the pace at which he spoke, could cite past history and past candidates off the top of his head.

How do you keep all that in your brain? I wondered upon meeting him.

I think Stagg was excited about my campaign because he liked seeing someone new in the party. He took me to his house, a beautifully decorated 1940s brick bungalow with handsome built-in bookshelves, and pulled out a big drawer filled with mailers from past candidates. One by one, he pulled out the leaflets from his collection and asked me to analyze their effectiveness.

"Look at their color schemes. Look at the fonts they use. Look at the graphics. Where do you put pictures? What kind of pictures? Who should be in those pictures? Look at buzzwords. Look at words that are in bold. Try to pick up on what works here. Tell me what's happening in this mailer."

He made me look at details I had previously not paid much attention to and helped me understand that each piece had been crafted to appeal to a particular group. I had previously thought that you simply provided a short biography that listed some of the issues you cared about and went with whatever colors you were using for your campaign.

"Oh, you are *so* naïve," Stagg said with dismay. "Let me show you." He pulled out a Republican campaign flyer. "When Jim Gibbons has a picture with firefighters, police officers, and military personnel, yes, it targets those groups, but it's also designed to appeal to conservatives who like seeing guys in uniform behind a candidate," he explained. "By contrast, Democrats use pictures to convey their values: education, middle-class families, minorities, unions, and the like."

Then he identified numerous people in the local party whom I needed to contact.

"Yeah, well, the party hasn't exactly been the most helpful," I grumbled.

"I know, but these are things you have to do," he announced. "So get over yourself, suck it up, and play the role."

I mentioned that I never got invited to any of the party-sponsored events.

"Of course you don't. You weren't exactly invited to this dance. You showed up on your own, so yeah, they're not going to welcome you."

I felt heartsick. It's one thing to suspect that you're deliberately being excluded, and another to have someone else confirm it. Realizing that the Democrats had decided that I wasn't part of the club was like finding out that the Tooth Fairy, the Easter Bunny, and Santa Claus weren't real. It was as if one of my closest friends had died. I had been told my entire life that the Democrats were the white hats, the ones who saved the day, who fought against poverty and for civil rights. Now all I could see was them fighting me. I couldn't understand why they didn't see things the way I did, and why a party that I had always thought invited everyone into the fold was excluding those who weren't as elitist as its leaders suddenly appeared to be.

In retrospect, I'd wished I had listened more closely to Stagg's advice instead of taking what I perceived to be the party's snub so personally. If I was going to jump into this game, I simply had to play by its rules. Of course, my being overly sensitive didn't change the fact that with a very few exceptions, I was basically on my own. Luckily, Stagg provided the support I wasn't finding in the places I'd expected.

"Here's what we're going to do," he announced. "I am going to tell you about all these events and when they're happening, and I'm going to feed them to you, and you're going to go anyway. These are public events, so they can't keep you out. Then have fun screwing with the party insiders by asking them whether they forgot to invite you." I knew he was kidding, but it was fun to visualize how that conversation would play out.

I left Stagg's home with fifty things to do that I hadn't been doing because I hadn't known any better. I couldn't wait to share my newfound knowledge with my class.

11

Politicos in the Making

* ★ ★ ★ ★ ★ ★ ★ ★ ★ ★ ★ ★ ★ ★ ★ ★ ★ ★

"I cannot believe that my child is watching CNN," Brent Thompson told me. Though he was a right-wing conservative who is hugely pro-NRA and anti-abortion, he loved our campaign because of its impact on his daughter. Laura, a natural leader in the classroom whose smarts and confidence had put her center stage, now sat at the dinner table and grilled her family with questions about the government.

"Considering the Bill of Rights and the Second Amendment, could an individual have an F-14 with rocket-launching missiles?" she asked her family quite seriously one night.

"What? What are you talking about?" her father sputtered.

"Well, that's bearing arms. Where do you draw the line?"

Her father was quite pleased that his daugher would come home and push the envelope, making him defend his way of thinking. She wasn't spouting anything I had said. She was simply playing devil's advocate, which we did in class all the time. Instead of handing my students answers,

I had them battle things out among themselves and come to their own decisions. In the process, they became better thinkers.

Though some kids participated in the campaign after school, it became the core part of our social studies—a lesson that never ended. Since the district didn't have enough money to buy us social studies textbooks, I handed out the newspaper, talked about current events, and related them either to democracy, voting, the government, or issues facing our country today. The kids looked up the terms they didn't understand—there are a lot of weird ones when it comes to government—and talked about what they meant. Sometimes even I wasn't sure.

"So let's find out," I told them.

When kids realize that you don't have all the answers and that we need to look up things together, it creates a sense of safety in the room. They realize that it's okay not to know everything, and they learn to be very resourceful.

We continued to march through the history of mankind—from cavemen drawings to the Vietnam War—bringing it all to life rather than relying on textbooks. During the segment on ancient Egypt, I told the kids that we were going to make mummies.

"We'll be dissecting an animal by-product, so you'll need to bring herbs and spices to preserve your mummy, and dental floss, tweezers, and needles to sew it up."

Every kid in the class skipped right over the word "by-product," assumed we would be dissecting animals, and promptly freaked out. I didn't say a word. Instead I passed around latex gloves. "You'll need to wash your hands before lunch," I said dramatically. "I don't want anyone getting sick."

I played it up as much as I could. When I finally walked

in with the box of bratwurst, most of the students were ready to revolt rather than dissect the mouse or frog they had envisioned. They began slicing through the skins of their bratwurst with equal measures of relief and enthusiasm. After they had taken out the organs (the middle of the bratwurst) and stored them in a baby-food jar, they stuffed the open cavity with herbs and stitched the skins closed. They wrapped their sausages in toilet paper and decorated the outside with faces. Then they wrote the mummies' life stories and learned some hieroglyphics to emblazon their sarcophagi for eternity with ancient symbols and words.

The project had taken several weeks, but the ground outside was still frozen and hard, so burying our mummies had to wait. We stacked them in shoe boxes on top of the bright yellow cubbies at the back of the room until we could dig up our burial site. Not surprisingly, the mummies began to smell.

Normally when folks walk into my classroom, they breathe in deeply and say, "Mmm, it smells so nice in here. What is that?" My big secret—Glade Plug-ins—is well known to almost anyone who teaches sweaty children. Sixth graders are notorious for having interesting odors. Each year, as spring hit and they returned from recess glowing with perspiration, I'd have to have The Talk. Without using any names, of course, I discussed how important it was for all of us to be able to live in the same room together without gagging. This always prompted some chuckles. Then I pointed out how important it was for me to shower each morning, put on deodorant, clean socks, and, yes, clean underwear. "And believe it or not, it's important for you to do that, too!" I concluded. "In fact, it's a good idea for you to remember to brush your teeth every morning and every night, wash your face, and make sure your clothes are clean, even if you need to do the sniff test." The giggling was always pronounced by this point. But if we didn't have this discussion, my room quickly became almost unbearable no matter what I did.

Unfortunately, however, even my favorite Hawaiian Breeze plug-in was no match for our ripening mummies. On a late winter day when my room was particularly unbearable, our principal came through for a visit. I could see her standing in the back of the room grimacing because of the smell. Penny finally couldn't take it any longer.

"Ms. Cahill, I'm sorry to interrupt your lesson, but I need to have a talk with your class," she announced before launching into the "You have *got* to take a shower every day, and ask your mom or dad to get you some deodorant" lecture. I raised my hand and tried to stop her.

"Don't interrupt," she directed. As I put my hand down, the giggling started. A few of the kids tried to let her know what was up, but she gave them the "be-quiet-until-I'm-done-speaking" look. The giggles escalated as she continued.

"You must wear clean underwear and socks. I mean, this room is seriously unbearable," she continued, becoming visibly frustrated with my poorly behaved class. "I don't know how you guys can stand being in here."

By this point, the kids were falling out of their desks and howling with laughter. I could barely contain my own amusement. Finally I said, "Mrs. LaBranch, it's not the kids, it's the mummies."

She stared at me like I was an alien. "You have what in this room?"

The kids were now screaming and crying with laughter as they pointed to the mummies on the back shelf.

"It's been too cold to bury our mummies, so we've been living with them till the ground thaws out," I finally explained.

Penny shook her head as she walked out. "Ms. Cahill, I don't know about you. Dead mummies. What in the world? Get them out of here and get some air fresheners, for goodness' sakes!"

My principal might not have liked the stinky mummies, but because of hands-on involvement, my kids sure did. The campaign continued to excite them for exactly the same reason. Every day before launching into our social studies unit, we spent ten minutes on an election update. I also used the time to keep the committees on task.

"Where are we with T-shirts, guys?" I asked. "Has anybody called the printer? Do we know when we need to go pick those up?"

Before ordering our T-shirts, my managerial committee had determined how many to print. As always, I gave them information and then let them make the call.

"Here is how much money we have. How many T-shirts do you think we should buy? Remember, we want to order buttons and signs, too."

Once we had our campaign paraphernalia, my students accompanied me to the union halls, senior centers, and other kinds of public organizations with "Cahill for Congress" proudly splashed across their chests. They also helped out on Candidate Days, which were often held at malls. On one particular Candidate Day, we set up our table at what used to be the hippest (and pretty much the only) mall when I was in high school. Park Lane Mall was no longer cool. Filled with odd stores that couldn't afford a space in the larger and much swankier new mall south of town, it was often a ghost town, though the new movie theater next door did draw some people.

Ingrid, Ardean, and Brent had stopped by to work our table, which was well stocked with buttons, signs, and T-shirts—and our handy Folgers donation can—as I watched. Ingrid usually just asked passersby if they wanted a button, but Ardean and Brent operated as a very outgoing and persuasive duo.

"Do you have any questions about any of the candidates?" they asked couple after couple.

Usually the people grinned, wondering what the boys were getting at. More often than not, they entertained their inquiry. "Well, not really, but what do you mean?"

"Well, we've asked our teacher to run for Congress and we're running her campaign," the boys explained unabashedly. "So we were wondering if you had any questions, because we just happen to have the candidate right over here."

I'd wave and smile, and sometimes the couple would come over to our table to donate money. If they expressed interest in a T-shirt, the boys jumped into salesman mode.

"What size can we get you? Are you sure you don't need two? How about a button? Those are often collectors' items years from now, you know."

Ingrid, who was better at organizing than dealing with the public, let the boys work the crowd. Once the deal had been sealed, she handed them whatever they needed or made sure that the money went into the coffee can.

As always, the kids counted their take in class the next day. Then we moved into our math lesson and jumped elbow deep into converting fractions to decimals and then into percentages. A group of students at a table in the back

searched through the newspaper for anything with percentages, decimals, or fractions. As they threw numbers at me,
I'd write them on the overhead projector. Then I had the
kids convert them. As they explained their logic and provided step-by-step instructions on what I was to write on
the overhead's glass, a team of checkers either agreed or disagreed. Then the phone rang.

Laura politely interrupted. "The Douglas County Democrats want you to come and speak to them this evening," she
said. I looked over in surprise. Douglas County is home to
the quaint towns of Minden and Gardnerville, which sit at
the base of Job's Peak an hour south of Reno. It's ranchland
there, with one high school, one McDonald's, one Raley's
grocery store, and friendly faces that are mostly all-white
and very Republican.

"Are you sure?" I asked.

"I'm positive," she replied in her thirty-year-old serious
voice.

"Hmmm . . . that's interesting," I mused, unaware that I
was speaking out loud.

"Why do you say that, Ms. Cahill?" Ardean chirped.

Never one to miss an opportunity, I said, "Well, okay, let's
talk about percentages. Douglas County has a very small
percentage of Democrats, so I guess I'm surprised they even
have a Democratic Club."

"Why would they have a small percentage of Democrats?" asked Laura.

I had to walk a fine line between my own opinions and
trying to stay nonjudgmental for the sake of education.

"Typically, small rural towns tend to be more conservative
in their way of life, values, and politics," I answered.

"But why is that?" asked Ardean.

I wondered if the children from Republican families

were thinking, *That's easy, they're just smarter.* As a child, I would have made that smart-ass comment if the conversation had been about a mostly Democratic community. Luckily, none of the kids went there.

Ardean saved me from having to answer his last question by posing another. "Ms. Cahill, how many Democrats are there in Douglas County?"

With a sense of relief, I said, "Frank, why don't you look that up on the Internet real quick and let us know, and we'll see if we can figure out the math of Douglas County." Frank, being very introverted, loved the chance to tap his talent for computers and show me what he could do. In no time I had a report. "Ms. Cahill, there are about 40,000 people in Douglas County. Actually there are exactly 41,392."

"Thanks, Frank. Okay, let's use your estimated number to figure out about how many Democrats there are. That way we can figure out if speaking there will be worth my time and decide whether I should go."

The power to determine where I would drive and who I'd speak with left my class giddy with excitement. I had Frank search Google for any information he could find about Republicans and Democrats in Douglas County. He proudly reported that the ratio of Republicans to Democrats there was two to one. We hadn't gotten to ratios yet, but this was a fairly good time to address the topic. I posed the question to the whole class.

"How can we find out how many people belong to each party if we know that there's a two-to-one ratio of Republicans to Democrats?"

Someone yelled out, "Divide them into thirds, then two thirds will be Republicans and one third will be Democrats."

A number of children raced to figure how many people

made a third and how many made two thirds. Not everyone did the calculations, but that was okay. I'm usually fine with that as long as they stay tuned in. Children will often struggle if they have to copy down a concept, particularly if they have dysgraphia. This writing disability requires them to expend so much energy just to recall and form the shapes of letters or numbers that they can't concentrate on anything else that's being said, and they usually shut down as a result.

I wrote on the overhead as the students who had chosen to actively participate defended their math to their classmates. There's a time for expecting kids to come up with a product that shows what they know, and there's a time to share mathematical thinking strategies.

"Okay, I've got it," Laura said. "If you divide 40,000 by three, you'll get 13,333.33. That gives you one third that makes up the Democrats, and if you add 13,333.33 plus 13,333.33 you'll get 26,666.66. That's how many Republicans there are."

"That's not the only way to do it!" Ardean countered.

"Okay," I said. "Show me how you did it, Ardean."

Ardean conferred with Frank, who opted to take the lead. "Well, if you remember back to when we were multiplying fractions by whole numbers, it means you're finding a part of something. So we wanted to find one third of 40,000 and the word *of* is a signal word that means multiplication," he said pointing to the chart of math signal words on the wall in front of him. Signal words are important because they help kids figure out what to do when confronted with a mathematical word problem.

"So, we multiplied 40,000 by one third," Frank continued. "That means you have to put 40,000 over one, because anything over one equals itself. Then you multiply straight across: 40,000 over one times one third equals 40,000 over three, which then means we have an improper fraction (the numerator or top number is greater than the denominator). So we have to divide the numerator 40,000 by the denominator three, which gives us 13,333.33."

"Isn't that the same as the way I did it?" asked Laura.

"Yes and no," replied Frank. "We came up with a fraction, not a decimal."

Either way, I was delighted to see that they not only understood these mathematical concepts, they could also explain them. Then the conversation turned to what to do with .33 or one third of a person before the kids eventually agreed that though it was funny to talk about, it wasn't realistic and should be dropped.

"So now that we know that there are one third, .33, or 13,333 Democrats out of 40,000 people living in Douglas County, what do you guys think? Should I go tonight?"

"Well, I hope you go because I said you'd be there," Laura quickly replied. "Sorry, but you had an opening in your calendar, and you need to visit as many people as possible. Even if Douglas County only has about 13,000 Democrats, they are voters and they should get to see you as much as any of the other sixteen counties."

"Yeah," agreed Paul. "You probably should figure out a way to get to all seventeen counties."

In a picture-perfect campaign I'd visit every county in Nevada, probably wearing my cowgirl boots and Rockies Jeans, and carrying a shotgun for a photo opportunity. Ultimately, however, this was a numbers game. I didn't have anywhere near the $1 million-plus required to run a highly competitive campaign. So I would figure out how to reach the maximum number of people who might potentially vote for me while taking into account the time and cost required to get there. I'd go to the counties I could easily reach after the school day had ended, and try to get to Clark County (Las Vegas), where Democrats actually outnumbered Republicans, as often as I could. While Douglas didn't exactly have a wealth of Democrats, it was only an hour away, so the class won.

"Okay, I'll go," I said.

Laura, the ever-responsible secretary, reminded me to take along some buttons and a couple of signs.

"Oh, and don't forget the Cahill for Congress Coffee Can for donations," Frank chimed in. "We need the money to get you to all of those seventeen counties."

As we all laughed, I thought about how observing the kids' thought processes and listening to them justify their thinking is exactly why I love teaching. I don't consider myself a teacher as much as I do a facilitator. I just guide them along the way by asking questions and demonstrating that it's more important to be "passionately curious," as Einstein said about himself, than to have all the answers. Curiosity, however, could be a double-edged sword when the focus turned to the issues in general, and to my opinion about them in particular.

"I want to know what you think about abortion," Brooks asked me after school when we were alone in the classroom. Brooks was a talented athlete whose life had been devastated when his parents' marriage had dissolved and his father had walked out. He was clearly trying to sort out his own sentiments on the subject and was determined to ferret out mine.

"Why do you want to know that?" I asked.

"Well, because I really wonder what you think."

"I can respect that you and I spend a lot of time together since we're all a pretty close-knit group and I can see why you might want to know where I stand personally, but I don't think it would benefit you to know that," I replied. "I think it's more important for you to go home and talk to your mom."

"I won't get you in trouble," he pleaded. "I won't tell, I promise."

"Thank you, but I'm not going to tell you what I think, because my opinion doesn't teach you to think for yourself. Your opinion is important to me, though."

"I guess I don't think it's right," he said.

"Okay, why do you not think it's right?"

"Because it's a baby and I can't imagine anybody wanting to kill a baby. That could have been me."

"Then that's what's important and I respect your thoughts," I told him.

He still looked frustrated, but I wasn't going to share my beliefs on the topic with him or any other student. We teachers hold much more power and influence over our students than we sometimes realize. And kids really do pay attention. Not all the time, obviously—there were days I don't think anybody heard a word I said. But at other times students will sit up, lean forward, and take it all in, and you don't know how that will spin them. Years later they come back to you and say, "You know, there was this one time you said this to me" and you don't even recall what you meant. So to me, the promise I had made to my students' parents not to discuss controversial issues was sacred.

12

Honor Bound

★ ★ ★ ★ ★ ★ ★ ★ ★ ★ ★ ★ ★ ★ ★ ★ ★ ★

No campaign is spared its share of dirty pool. Even so, I figured that a campaign run by a group of sixth graders and
their teacher would be exempt. I was wrong.

In school, we get notices of contests in our mailboxes all
the time. When I read the flyer about a contest asking students to write about why we as citizens should vote, I didn't
care that it was sponsored by the Washoe County Republican Party. Since it provided a good opportunity for kids to
express their ideas and since it tied in well with our election
project, I had my students write one-page essays on the
topic "What it means to be an American and have the right
to vote." Then they edited their work for spelling, punctua-
tion, and grammar, and we submitted all the essays to the
contest.

The winner was to be announced during a candidate
event held at an older mall called Shopper's Square. The
candidates' tables had been set up along the passageways in
front of odd little specialty stores that sold sewing materials
and the like. The announcement of the winner—which

most of the kids, along with their parents, had come to hear—was to be made by a radio DJ named Rusty Humphries, a wannabe Rush Limbaugh bully on his local radio pulpit. Those right-wing shock jocks always bug me because they never have a real conversation or let anybody who doesn't totally agree with them express themselves. They run over them, cut them off, call them idiots, and make sure they never get the last word. This event proved no exception.

Though the announcement had been scheduled for noon, Humphries's candidate interviews ran late. It got to be 1 p.m., then 1:30 p.m., and still no annoucement had been made. Eventually, a bunch of the kids had to leave, their parents unwilling to waste any more of their weekend. Finally it was time.

"The winner is Rachel G," Humphries proclaimed, adding in a disgusted voice, "from Miss Cahill's class."

I suppose he couldn't bear the fact that a student from the class of a Democratic candidate had won. I went up and accepted on her behalf.

"I apologize, but Rachel has already left," I said. "Her family was told, as were we, that this would be announced at noon."

That ticked Humphries off. I guess he didn't want to look like he had been rude or out of line by running late, so he tried to divert his public's attention by turning it right around on Rachel.

"What a slacker," he said. "Can you believe she didn't even show up for her own award ceremony?"

His snub earned him some cheap laughs, even though the delay and my twelve-year-old student's departure had been his fault.

"On her behalf, thank you for the award. I will let her

know she won this, of course," I said when he handed me the award. "But she was here on time when this was supposed to have been announced."

The next day I let the class know that we had a winner in the essay contest.

"We should all be really proud," I said. "That's an amazing feat considering how many kids from different schools submitted essays."

Then I congratulated Rachel and everyone cheered. When I reminded them that she had won a class tour of the governor's mansion in Carson City, Nevada's capital, located forty-five minutes away, they cheered again. "Way to go, Rachel!" they yelled, excited about the prospect of a field trip that would get them out of school for a day. A pretty girl whose hairdresser mother probably styled her picture-perfect hair every day before school, Rachel just smiled in her typically quiet and humble way.

I had picked up Rachel's award, but when I called to make arrangements for the rest of the prize, my call was not returned. Neither were the six or seven other phone messages I left for the Washoe County Republicans, who were supposed to coordinate the visit.

"I'm very sorry," said the volunteers fielding my calls, usually retired people who sat in the office to answer the phone and hand out literature to anybody who walked in. "I've let the chairwoman, Earlene Forsythe, know that you've called over and over. I'll leave another message for her."

My subsequent handwritten notes and e-mails pointing out how unfair withholding this prize was to the child met with the same lack of response. I went down to Republican headquarters and asked to speak with the chairwoman. She was never in the office, which is pretty typical. Party chairs don't actually work there. The office exists to get voters registered, and to have a place for candidates to leave their literature, as well as a place for meetings in the evenings. So, it didn't surprise me that I didn't find her in. Still, I thought that maybe if I showed up physically and she was told that I had actually inquired in person, I might start getting somewhere.

"This little girl won. And she's twelve. How do you not honor that?" I told the mostly elderly headquarter volunteers.

Though they sympathized, nothing happened.

"Have you heard anything from them yet?" Rachel asked periodically.

"No, honey, I'm sorry," I answered each time. "I'm trying."

"Well, I don't understand. That's kind of lame that they give out a prize and then don't let you have it."

Unable to think of anyone else to approach, in a last-ditch effort I tried my opponent's then-wife, Dawn Gibbons, a powerful Nevada legislator in her own right. I'd seen Dawn, who looks like a bubbly, peppy fifty-year-old Jessica Simpson, on a TV newscast with her husband. She just seemed to have such kind eyes. Besides, I kept hearing that she was a closet Democrat because she was pro-union, pro-choice, and pro-woman, and voted her conscience instead of the Republican party line.

My late-night e-mail laid out the details of the contest and my unsuccessful attempts to secure the prize that had been promised. "I feel really odd coming to you, but I know what a good person you are," I wrote. "I don't know who else to ask. Please help us."

I knew from Ron Seckler, one of my vice principals, that when Dawn's son had been in middle school, the state legislator had shown up one day in sweats, a T-shirt, tennies, and a ponytail, with a bucket of cleaning supplies.

"I would like to give some of my time to the school today," she announced. "Would it be okay if I went around and cleaned things up?"

The school principal looked shocked. He was probably even more shocked when she headed to the bathrooms that day, got on her hands and knees, scrubbed the floors, and then asked what else she could do. I'm sure she was sending a message. She wanted to say, "I care about the schools and I'm not sure how to help, but I'm ordinary and not above you all. I'm down here in the trenches with you and I want this to be a good place for kids."

I concluded my e-mail to Dawn Gibbons by saying that I didn't think it was right to deny Rachel the prize she had won for her class. "I'm sorry I'm the Democratic candidate, but don't punish my student for it. She rightfully earned that award."

Dawn's response was as immediate as it was sweet.

> I'm so embarrassed and so sorry. I can't explain why no one has been in touch with you or returned your calls. Please allow me to pay for a bus so your students can come to Carson City. I'll set up a tour and a luncheon at the governor's mansion and then we'll bring them over to the state legislature and take them onto the floor, where they'll be recognized and put into the official record.

Despite my immense gratitude, I couldn't help wondering whether her response was due to her being a good person or because it would play well. It was probably a bit of both. Jim Gibbons's stance on education had never been perceived as particularly strong, and Dawn counterbalanced that in her work. Upping the ante on our prize would make her look good. The fact that she'd be hosting her husband's opponent wouldn't hurt either.

I made the kids dress up for the field trip.

"Pretend you're going to a wedding or an important religious service," I told them. I wanted the girls in skirts and blouses or dresses.

"You will look like ladies," I told them. "We are going to present ourselves in a way that is highly respectable. This is a huge honor, and we need to dress appropriately. If you're going to go, you're going to look like you belong there."

The boys had to wear khakis—no jeans allowed—along with a button-down shirt and tie, no ifs, ands, or buts. They were mortified.

"Do we *have* to?"

"Yes. You're going to out of respect for the legislature."

"I don't have a tie," a couple of them said.

"Borrow one. Buy one. Ask your dad. Ask your neighbor. I don't care, but you find one," I replied.

The morning of the trip, the kids looked as spiffy as I'd ever seen them. We took a bus down to Carson City and went to the legislature first. One of Dawn's assistants met us and took us on a tour of the silver-domed building, a tribute to the fact that Nevada is the Silver State. The kids thought it was all pretty slick. They were amazed at the volume of information and paperwork in the huge research rooms where all the law books and records are stored. And they were particularly impressed that a whole group of people who are not legislators at all—secretaries, runners, researchers, and staff members—actually runs the place and keeps it going year-round.

From there we were taken to Dawn Gibbons's office. The legislator had a bag of cookies wrapped in cellophane and tied with a bow for each child, which blew my mind. She would surprise me again years later when she took me to a cattle-branding breakfast fund-raiser out in the desert north of Reno. In a scene that looked like it was right out of the 1800s, the camp cook dished up eggs, potatoes, and pancakes as cowboys branded and castrated calves before giving them their shots.

A cowboy came up to Dawn and me. "Would you gals like some Rocky Mountain Oysters [otherwise knows as bull testicles]?" he joked.

Another cowboy said, "Mrs. Gibbons, we met before. Do you remember me?"

She paused and then said, "Oh, I'm sorry. I didn't recognize you with your clothes on."

I laughed, loving that this state legislator was so down to earth that she could make a cowboy blush with a joke.

Of course, standing in Dawn's office with my students, I had no way of knowing that she and I would become friends. I just knew that I liked the humanness I saw in her. After posing for a group picture with her, we headed down to the floor of the legislature, which was in session, and took our seats in the Assembly Chambers as Dawn headed to the dais.

"I want it put into the official record that Miss Cahill's sixth-grade class from Sarah Winnemucca Elementary is here," she said into the microphone. "They've been running a Congressional campaign. And they have an award-winning essayist here today who wrote about why we should vote."

As Dawn returned to join us, the whole assembly clapped for my students, who stood up to be recognized.

"I would love to serve here," I said in a low voice. "This is where you lift the education of kids in Nevada."

I'd more or less been talking to myself, but Dawn overheard.

"Well then, you should run."

"I would kind of be picking on your family, wouldn't I?" I answered. "I'd have to run against you!"

"I won't be here forever. If I'm not here, someday you should run."

First, however, I had to get through this campaign. That was challenge enough.

13

The Perils of Running

* * * * * * * * * * * * * * * * * * * *

Life quickly escalated from difficult to daunting. That spring,
I was forced to have a hernia operation. I'd planned to be out
of commission only three days. The surgeon, however, acci-
dentally severed a nerve during the surgery and then sutured
another one. The pain that followed was excruciating—
worse than a cesarean—but I'd been an athlete, so I tried to
tough it out. After two weeks, however, I was still in horrible pain and it just wouldn't go away. Eventually, a second
surgery was scheduled once my surgeon determined that an
entrapped nerve must have gotten caught in a suture. The
operation to kill the nerves that were signaling nonstop pain
finally solved the problem.

I had just returned to work when a man calling himself
"the Wizard" started phoning.

"You did such a good job," he said the first time, referring
to a recent campaign appearance I had made. "But yellow
really isn't your color." In addition to commenting on my
V-neck sleeveless sweater set, he critiqued my eye makeup.

That's so creepy, I thought with a pronounced sense of

unease. The fact that he refused to identify himself creeped me out even more. *Who is this guy?*

"Just wanted to let you know the Wizard's cheering for you!" he announced the second time. "I'll be doing my magic." He concluded the call with a nod toward the wardrobe he had previously criticized. "Much better job on the clothes," he affirmed.

His tone of voice was always happy, excited and supportive, but his calls still freaked me out. *Why hasn't he introduced himself at the events that he's obviously attended? Why does he want to remain anonymous?* I wondered. *And what kind of name is the Wizard? What's that supposed to mean?*

The calls got stranger.

"I know you're going to win, because I've looked into my magic ball, and Jim Gibbons is going to go poof and disappear," he predicted.

Oh my god, what if he hurts Jim Gibbons? I thought. *What if he kills Jim Gibbons so I can win? What if he's that crazy?*

I thought about calling the police, but figured they would simply conclude that *I* was the one who was nuts. Instead, from then on each time I was in a crowd, I'd look around and think, *Who is it who's looking at me?*

He called enough that my children, as well as my students, who now answered my cell phone in class as part of their media duties, began to know his voice.

"If it's the Wizard, she's absolutely not available," they coached each other, and then put him off firmly but politely when he phoned. "I'm sorry, Mr. Wizard. She's busy." As soon as the Wizard was off the line, they always laughed. They thought the name was really funny, but the guy gave me the major creeps. The calls—and the caller—bordered on obsessive. I wondered why he liked me so much. Was he truly a supporter or was he a freak who had become overly attached to me? I didn't know what his motives were. Unnerved, I wondered if I was being stalked.

The Wizard wasn't the only disturbing man in my life. A few months prior, my family and I had relocated from our two-bedroom, one-bath apartment. We had needed to move for months, since the toilet overflowed constantly and almost always at night.

"Mommy, I gotta go, I gotta go!" my three little ones would beg.

What was I going to do? The maintenance guy refused to work after hours, and my kids had to go to the bathroom. So I'd dress them all in their warm sweats and we'd run across the parking lot down to the sports bar on the corner to use the bathroom. That was really nice.

"Don't sit on the seat, honey," I would remind them before getting out of there as quickly as possible.

Then Derrick, my manipulative and ungenerous boyfriend at the time, offered to pull some money out of the stock market and invest in a house that I could rent.

"You and the kids can get out of this apartment and it'll be a home where they can play in the front yard."

I was beside myself.

"Are you kidding?" I exclaimed. "Oh my god, that is the nicest thing anyone has ever done for me. Okay—thank you—holy cow!"

So we went out and started looking at real estate and found a clean, tiny house in a downtown Reno neighborhood that's attractive but very transient. Derrick put down $5,000 on the two-bedroom Mediterranean-style house with a backyard filled with weeds and goat heads—horrible, small round plant seeds with two sharp thorns that are incredibly painful to step on. The mortgage was covered by my rent payments.

"How about if we paint and get the backyard land-scaped?" I asked after the kids and I had moved in.

"Well, you can do that if you want to pay for it," he answered.

"If I want to pay for it? I'm sorry, you own the house. You're the one who will profit when you sell," I replied.

"I think I've already done you and your kids a favor by buying the house for you," he retorted.

Any gratitude I had initially felt hit the Dumpster. "Buying it for me? For me?" I raged at Derrick, who had obviously reverted to form. "So my name is on the title?"

"Hell, no, your name isn't on the title."

"Well, then please don't say you bought it for me."

Needless to say, the house didn't get painted and the backyard didn't get landscaped since we didn't have the money to do anything. So the kids were relegated to playing in the minute, manicured front yard. But our neighbors to the east were skinheads with swastika tattoos who were quite obviously dealing drugs. Thirty to forty visitors would pull up each day, go into the house, and come right back out. I remember being at the kitchen sink doing dishes one weekend when Kelton, Kennedy, and O'Keeffe were climbing the funny tree with huge leaves and pods like vanilla beans out front. To the kids, that tree seemed like something out of a fairy tale. To me, the scary house next door also seemed like something out of a fairy tale, and not in a good way. When I spotted even more tattooed wannabe Nazis parking their car in front of my house, I suddenly felt as if I couldn't breathe. I ran out the front door.

"Get inside now," I yelled at the kids as my neighbors flipped me off.

The place was even more out of control at night, with parties raging until one or two in the morning, complete with loud music, screaming, and bottles breaking. Still, the house we lived in was supercute and I figured that the renters next door wouldn't last forever. I even envisioned a time in the future when I might be able to buy the house from Derrick, so that my family would have a home to call our own. When I mentioned that to Derrick's son from his first marriage, who was only four years younger than I, he chuckled.

"Tierney, sometimes it's so heartbreaking."

"What do you mean?" I asked.

"First of all, I don't even know why my dad has you. It's unbelievable that you stay with him. You don't see things for what they are."

"What do you mean?" I repeated.

"Because what you really are is a renter he fucks."

I didn't know what to say.

"I know that sounds terrible, and I don't mean to hurt your feelings because you are so nice, but Tierney, he is not nice to you. He is not a nice person. He totally takes advantage of you. This house will never be yours."

His hurtful comments stung, but like icy water they woke me up and got me to start paying attention. *Maybe he's right,* I thought. Derrick had been about as unsupportive as possible during the campaign. I would tell him, "I'm sorry, I won't be around for dinner tonight, because I have this dinner to go to, and then I have to drive to Gardnerville and meet with the Douglas County Democrats." In response, he would demean me.

"This is a joke," he said. "I can't believe you're going through with this. It's such a waste of time. Why don't you do something important, like stay home and take care of your kids?"

When I didn't acquiesce and change my plans, he said, "Fine, I don't need to see you anyway."

His mean-spirited comments probably stemmed from insecurity. As a younger man he had been very good-looking. Now that he was getting older, drinking a lot, and looking unhealthy, he wasn't getting as much attention as he'd gotten in his younger years. My sudden visibility—along with my new packed schedule that made me a lot less available to him—clearly annoyed him.

Since Derrick wanted all eyes on him all the time, he said and did whatever it took to gain an audience. As much as he despised my campaign, he endorsed it publicly if he could somehow benefit from that exposure. One night he walked up to State Attorney General Frankie Sue Del Papa, whom he had met only in passing.

"Hey! How's it going?" he said to her, relying on his best used-car-salesman approach.

"Who are you?" she asked.

"Oh, yeah, I'm Tierney Cahill's boyfriend. She's great. Isn't she great?"

He thrived on those contacts. Then we'd go home and he would mock me.

"You're so out of your element here. They're walking all over you. They're laughing behind your back."

"Oh my god, how can you talk to me like that?" I'd answer in disgust.

"Hey, I'm trying to help you out here. I can't help it if you can't see this for what it is."

Our interactions worsened over time. During one argument, I sent the kids upstairs once he began throwing our belongings in the trash in a drunken rage. O'Keeffe came back down in tears.

"Can you please stop yelling at my mommy?" my youngest asked.

Derrick looked at him. "You know, there's a reason your dad left your mommy," he replied.

That particular low point hit near the end of our seven years together. My best friend, Stacey, challenged me about the relationship when it got ugly, which it so often did.

"Tierney Cahill, Cahill for Congress, I cannot believe that you would tolerate this in your life," she told me. "As stubborn and ornery as you are, I cannot believe that you put up with this."

I knew the relationship should be ended. I just didn't have it in me to take that on, too.

Hiding from one problem didn't prevent others. In mid summer, just a week after my new class had started, our new house was broken into. I didn't immediately perceive that anything was amiss when I got home from school. I dropped my stuff at the door and visited in the living room with Derrick's nineteen-year-old daughter, who was there with a friend of hers. Suddenly I noticed that the back door in the kitchen was ajar.

"That wasn't open when you got here, was it?" I asked.

"Yeah, it was."

"Oh no!" I exclaimed. I knew then that something wasn't right.

A quick survey revealed that the window in the black-and-white art-deco bathroom was wide open and the screen had been yanked off. I noticed that the dresser drawers in the bedroom had been pulled out. I started looking around more carefully to see if anything was missing. That's when I noticed that the box by the front door with all our campaign materials was gone. Our T-shirts, our handouts, our but-tons, all the materials that we walked the precincts with had been stored in that one box. When we'd go canvassing, the students from my class along with my three kids would line up and I'd dress them all in T-shirts. At the end of the day, we'd put the T-shirts back in the box, along with our literature. The campaign box never moved. It always stayed right there by the door.

Further investigation revealed that though my jewelry box hadn't been taken, a ring that my grandmother, who had since passed away, had given me as a college graduation present was missing. *Oh, god, not that!* I thought. A wooden box from the 1800s with tiny weights that a miner had once used to measure gold and the like was also gone. The cool old oak box had been my dad's, and was one of the few items of his that I had.

I burst out crying. Unused to seeing tears from their mom, Kelton, Kennedy, and O'Keeffe started crying too. Finally I composed myself enough to call the police. Since there were black imprints left from the dirty hands of whoever had crawled through the bathroom window, I figured that dusting for fingerprints would potentially reveal the culprit's identity.

"They're not clean," the Reno policeman said after several attempts to pull a smudged print. "It's probably someone who's addicted to drugs and is looking for things to sell quickly at a thrift or pawn store. I'm sure it didn't have anything to do with your campaign."

"Then why would they take my campaign material?" I asked.

"Well, it was near the door. Maybe they needed a box to throw stuff into."

That made sense, and I almost bought it.

That night, we all climbed in my bed as usual to read one of the Lemony Snicket books together. Though it was always a battle to get the tribe back into their own beds, I enjoyed the pile of little people snuggling in for a good read at the end of a busy day. This time, however, was different. They were really scared. The boys were worried that someone might come back and try and get in their basement window. Though Kennedy's small room was just on the other side of the bathroom by the stairs, she didn't want to stay by herself. I can't say that I felt all that serene either.

This tiny house has so many potential entrances, I thought, looking at the French doors in my bedroom that opened out onto the weed-ridden backyard.

"Can we please sleep with you, Mommy?" the kids pleaded.

"We can't all fit in my bed, but we could have a campout in Mommy's room. How would that be? Let's get out the sleeping bags. We'll go make hot cocoa and then jump in Mommy's bed for a couple of chapters. Then we'll all be together and there will be nothing to worry about."

The invitation was received with a resounding *"Yes!* Oh, thank you, Mommy!" The kids quickly unrolled their sleeping bags, placing one on each side of the bed and the third at the foot. I don't think any of us slept very well that first night or for the next few weeks until they returned to their beds. However, being together helped us all a lot. Even I felt comforted. The only drawback was trying to remember not to squash a kiddo if I had to get out of bed for anything.

The next morning I awoke early as usual to gather my things and make sure all the backpacks were ready to go before getting the kids up. Then I drove to school heavy with the knowledge that I would have to tell my students about the theft. I didn't want to be overly dramatic and worry them unnecessarily. My own children had that covered. But they did need to know, since this was going to hamper our walking efforts for a while.

"Why would anyone steal our campaign materials?" Brent asked in a voice that betrayed his sense of shock.

"The police officer didn't think this was related to the campaign at all," I explained.

They felt as bad for me as they did about the impact this would have on our campaign.

"I'm so sorry about the ring your grandmother gave you," said Julie. The other kids nodded in sympathy. Then Rocket asked, "What are we going to do about all of our campaign materials?"

"Well, what if we wrote letters to the editor and asked for people to please return our stuff?" Laura suggested. Our press secretary could delegate a list of tasks like a real pro. But when it came to this, her mini-adult attitude crumbled.

How cute is that? I thought. *She wants someone to be a good citizen and return what they've stolen.*

The kids were even more upset about the theft than they probably would have been ordinarily because we had already been dealing with the mysterious disappearance of a lot of our campaign signs, especially those in Republican neighborhoods.

"We put them up through the whole area," the kids told me. "We asked people and they said yes, we could put them in their yards. Then they disappeared."

"Yeah, I had to put ours in my upstairs bedroom window looking out on the front street, because every time we put one in the front yard, it got taken," Jacob confirmed.

I thought that was weird. The theft of our campaign material from my house made it seem even weirder.

"That's dirty and unfair. It's cheap politics," Laura

spouted, incensed that we had lost materials we could ill afford to replace. "You don't steal other people's signs and throw them away. And you sure don't break into their house."

Finally, she wrote to the editor of our local paper, describing the problem and explaining our need to have signs returned. "If you see anyone damaging any of Ms. Cahill's signs or have any information on the recent theft," Laura's letter concluded, "please notify the authorities."

Not everyone was as moved by this appeal as I was. In fact, Laura's letter triggered some inordinately harsh responses. One self-described "lifelong Democrat" opined that signs disappear in the course of every campaign. Cahill and her students should "get over it," the writer suggested. Then he concluded that, party affiliation notwithstanding, he could not vote for me. "The very idea of running for a national office as part of a sixth-grade school project is anathema to me and bespeaks of a certain lassitude in my own party."

In response, Laura's dad, the stern Republican NRA guy who had challenged me in the parent meeting, blasted the author of the letter.

I want to commend you on your heroic attack on the sixth-grade letter writer . . .

While most people would think it admirable for 11- and 12-year-old students to take on a class project that teaches them about our political system and the teamwork needed to accomplish common goals, you were able to see through this facade and label it simply as "complaining". . . .

In your letter you call yourself a "lifelong Democrat"; well, as a lifelong member of the human race, it would be wise for humanity to take anyone who uses the words "anathema," "bespeaks," and "lassitude" in a short paragraph and remove paper and pencil privileges for a long, long time. When the privileges are returned, perhaps you can tackle some antisocial preschooler.

I'm not sure if this exchange of letters to the editor is how Jim Gibbons found out that my house had been broken into or whether he saw the local news interview about the theft that materialized once Laura's letter was published. Either way, because I was a federal candidate he wrote a letter to the FBI asking them to investigate. So the FBI called to ask if I would come down to headquarters and tell them what had happened. The idea of going to the FBI was nerve-racking, but I knew my son Kelton, then in fifth grade, would love it so I took him along.

The FBI man, who had supposedly reviewed the file, interviewed us and then quickly concluded in a gruff way that it had probably been a random burglary.

"Yeah, but they took all of our campaign stuff," I said. "Don't you think that's a little weird?"

"There's nothing we can do," he said. "There are no fingerprints we can run. Since they did take some jewelry and valuables, it looks like it was not an attack on your campaign. And as far as your signs, we're sorry but that happens in races."

As we were getting ready to leave, my sweet, gentle-hearted son, who tends to live in a fantasy world, said, "Excuse me, sir, can I ask you a question, please? Is this where they keep the X-Files, because it would be really cool to see them."

"The X-Files!" the FBI investigator exclaimed. "Oh, no, son, we don't have anything that exciting here."

What a funny little kid, I thought as we left.

I didn't even question the FBI's conclusion, which had now been reached twice, that the theft had been completely unassociated with my campaign. Later, when we had moved out of Derrick's rental and I needed to change my voter-registration address, a frail old guy manning the desk whispered, "Oh, you're Cahill. I have to be quiet." Looking around to make sure no one was near, he said in a low voice, "I know about your house getting broken into."

"So you read about it in the paper or saw it on the news?" I asked, unnerved.

"No. You aren't the only one that's happened to. Other candidates trying to challenge powerful Republicans in the state have been targeted."

"What are you talking about?" I asked.

He mentioned a Democrat running for office whose campaign headquarters office had been broken into and a theft in another candidate's home.

"This is common. This is what they do."

I didn't understand. *This is what who does? They stole my box of buttons, handouts, and T-shirts. What does that do? Is that supposed to scare me?*

Still, his message was as disconcerting as his extreme nervousness. This veteran of local politics clearly didn't want anyone there to overhear what he was saying.

"The police don't think it was anything other than a random burglary," I countered. "They couldn't find any fingerprints."

"They never do," the old man said. "The guys who did this are professionals."

I didn't know what to think. He seemed like a credible man (he had worked in that office for twenty or thirty years). I was sure he knew lots of ins and outs, history, and gossip. On the other hand, maybe those elements had fused in his mind.

Of course, politically motivated professionals might have

been behind the theft, but my home wasn't the Watergate Hotel. I had no damning information against anybody. They didn't steal millions of dollars from me. Why would they bother? And who were "they"?

The burglary continued to distress my three little guys.

"Are all the windows locked, Mommy?" they asked at night. "Are all the doors locked?"

I couldn't blame them for being scared. We'd been getting nasty phone messages; the wizard dude, as the kids had dubbed him, kept calling; the entire Aryan nation was showing up next door; and now our home had been broken into. The next incident would make even our car feel unsafe.

I couldn't afford radio airtime, billboards, or television commercials, but I did have tape. So I duct-taped my campaign signs to the sides of my used maroon Chevy Lumina and turned the car into a rolling advertisement. One afternoon as we passed the colored fountain lights that my children liked to watch at the Peppermill, one of the larger and newer casinos located along Reno's main drag, a twenty-something guy in the backseat of the car next to us leaned out the window for a better look at my campaign sign.

"Democrat!" he screamed. "I hate Democrats. I wish all you fuckers would die."

Their eyes huge, Kelton, Kennedy, and O'Keeffe turned to look at this man, who was clearly trashed.

My littlest one, then six, started to cry. "Mommy, why does he want you to die?" he choked out through his tears.

"Honey, he's just a dumb kid," I answered, rolling up the window.

"You suck," the drunk continued to yell, his insults still audible through the now-closed window.

Feeling horrible that my three children had witnessed this, I turned on the radio and tried to comfort them.

"It's okay. There are weirdos in this world."

My words didn't help. Kennedy and O'Keeffe burst into fresh tears. Kelton, the oldest, was equally upset, but being ten, he didn't want to cry. So he got angry instead.

"Mom, I don't understand why you keep doing this!" he shouted. "This is so dumb. Why do you have to run for office? You're gone all the time. Our house has been broken into. Isn't this enough yet?"

"Mommy, please," the other two chimed in.

Not wanting to let them know how rattled I was, I put on a brave face and a smile, and assured them that everything was okay.

"He's just a confused, angry kid. Don't worry. He's been drinking."

Then I pulled out my trump card.

"Okay, we're fine, you guys. Let's go get a milk shake somewhere."

Even as I tried to downplay this latest trauma, I couldn't avoid the doubts that kicked in. In my effort to be the best candidate I could, I had missed too many of their games. You don't do that. I hoped the speech I had given earlier that week had been worth missing my youngest son's first-ever soccer game. "I'm going to kick the ball really, really hard for you, Mommy," he had said, lisping through the gap where his two front teeth used to be. I was sick that I hadn't gotten to see that.

Despite my being absent way too much, the kids were doing well. Kennedy had won an art contest, Kelton was excelling at baseball, and O'Keeffe had become a major attraction at T-ball, since every time he got up to bat he proclaimed to the crowd, "Are you ready? 'Cause I'm going to hit a home run!" It's not that he hit the ball that far, but he had figured out that as long as he didn't stop running, the other little guys probably couldn't catch and throw well enough to get him out. So he'd race around the bases with no intent of ever stopping and come into home sliding hard as if he'd just won the World Series for his team. He kept running even if he was thrown out, and then told everyone he still had his home run. If only success in life could be that way.

14

On the Ballot

★ ★ ★ ★ ★ ★ ★ ★ ★ ★ ★ ★ ★ ★ ★ ★ ★ ★ ★ ★

It was finally going to happen. We were going to be on the ballot. On May 11, I took the afternoon off—as half a personal day—to go file with the Secretary of State to run as a candidate for the House of Representatives in the Democratic primary. The kids were as excited as I was.

"Good luck! Good luck!" they cried as I left.

Just the week before, the campaign had been put on hold for the end-of-the-year science camp in Tahoe that my colleague and friend Todd and I took our classes to annually. The Great Basin Outdoor School rented Camp Galilee, located on the east side of the lake near Zephyr Cove, about ten miles from South Lake Tahoe, where the casinos are. Lake Tahoe is one of my most favorite places on the planet. The huge lake with its spectacular light-blue-and-emerald-green waters is flanked by massive granite boulders that the high school kids love to sunbathe on and then jump off when they need to cool down. The area is an outdoor person's dreamscape, offering hiking, bicycling, kayaking, skiing, sailing, and camping in wooded surroundings of over-whelming beauty.

Our camp had four dorms—two for girls and two for boys. We actually had more kids than there were beds for, so the adventurous ones stayed in tents. High school mentors supervised dorms and tents, while Todd and I stayed in the camp's small two-bedroom teachers' house. We all took our meals in a mess hall with long tables and benches, where we ate family style, passing the bowl of salad or spaghetti from one person to the next. The first couple of meals, the kids piled their plates high with food. But then we started weighing our waste at the end of each meal and graphing it. Before long they reminded one another at each meal not to take more than they really wanted to eat.

Each morning and evening, we gathered in an area that sloped down to the lake. The first night, sitting on old logs that had been cut in half and set up like tiered stadium seating, a university scientist taught us about the constellations and the mythology that surrounded them. The next day, we hiked around Spooner Lake as we looked at rock formations and discussed geological features that we'd studied all year. We also identified any wildlife we could find (mostly bugs and birds), as well as different plants and trees. The kids had booklets for sketching leaves or flowers, which they then labeled.

We crammed in as many activities that week as we could. Our students learned to use a compass by going on a treasure hunt, and to rely on their senses during a dark night hike. We met with a Native American tribe that owned the land in the area, listened to some of their tribal stories, and watched a number of their dances. We made solar ovens under the tutelage of conservation groups and then baked pizza and cookies in them. And we went out on a research boat to look at the phytoplankton and zooplankton that are causing spectacular Lake Tahoe to lose some of its renowned clarity. The scientists explained that because we're filling in and building on the wetlands, they're no longer filtering the water that makes its way to the lake. Carried by runoff from fertilized lawns and from the streets, more chemicals are winding up in the lake, which is impacting its chemical balance.

At the end of each day, the counselors, the naturalists, Todd, and I divvied out "character beads" to the kids in recognition of friendship, generosity, or other noteworthy behavior.

"Sasha, I saw that you were very hardworking and earnest today, and you learned your lesson," Todd noted during an evening campfire. "So, good job. Here's a bead for that." Clutching the coveted character bead, Sasha beamed. The bead quickly joined the others on her leather necklace, which also sported a piece of wood called a tree cookie that was about half an inch thick and decorated with her name and designs she had drawn.

As usual, the kids, many of whom had never been camping, bonded even more than they had during the school year and the campaign. And it was awesome to see how those who didn't excel academically thrived in that atmosphere. We returned home with a renewed sense of togetherness and purpose.

That month, having received the Best in Education in Washoe County award, the first major article about me hit the papers. Titled "A Real-Life Civics Lesson," it read, "A Reno teacher who has no money and no experience is running for Congress. This is actually a step up for Democrats. . . ." That about summed it up. Suddenly I started to feel like a real candidate.

Increasing appearances and the launch of our campaign website confirmed the feeling. I didn't even understand how to get a domain name or that I needed someone to host the site, but a friend of Derrick's who was a planner for the city of Sparks and very computer-literate set all that up for me. I told him what I needed on the site and he built it without charging me a cent. When it came to content, I went through the Democratic website and looked at its platform, and then basically provided my position on all its issues. An article would later mention that I was "almost word-for-word identical to the Democrats." In fact, with some minor changes I did believe in the party line.

I drove down to Carson City by myself. I had looked into taking the kids with me when I went to file, but my principal didn't think that burning a whole afternoon for me to sign papers would be a very good use of instructional time.

Incredibly nervous because I didn't know what I was doing, I walked into the Secretary of State's empty office and was promptly sent down to a rinky-dink office in the basement. I told the gal behind the counter that I was there to file. She got out the Declaration of Candidacy, which I signed and she notarized. Then she made me take an oath. I had to put up my right hand and promise to be ethical in campaigning and not get involved with any dirty politicking, which I found hysterical. I was determined to run a campaign devoid of any mudslinging, but that was definitely not the norm. I know very few candidates who actually adhere to that oath. If all the other states in this country have similar pledges, then that means the politicians have all broken their word before they even get into office.

I paid $300, an expense we had anticipated, from our campaign funds.

"Okay, I'll go and get the press," the woman who had made me official said.

Taken aback, I paused.

"What do you mean, 'get the press'?"

"The Capitol Bureau Journalism Office is right down here on this floor. Reporters from all the major newspapers in Nevada stay here in Carson City to cover what happens in the Capitol. We always bring them over to interview candidates when they file."

"Jesus! Interview me for what?" I exclaimed. "Wait!"

One of my biggest fears from the get-go had been how I would be presented in the media. Even though I couldn't imagine what could possibly come up that would hurt my family or be embarrassing, I fretted about it. I also worried that I wasn't the caliber of socialite that usually runs for office. The first article had worked out fine. But what if these journalists went on the attack? I could imagine them asking me, "What makes you think you're qualified to run?" *At least I dressed up to file,* I thought.

Before I knew it, journalists from the *Las Vegas Review Journal,* the *Las Vegas Sun,* the *Reno Gazette-Journal,* and the *Nevada Appeal,* Carson City's newspaper, had their pens poised over their tiny spiral notebooks. But while I was ready for the most intimate questions, the interview was fairly generic. I think the fact that I was a teacher afforded me some dignity and respect.

"Tell us a bit about your background and why you're running," they asked in voices devoid of emotion. It almost seemed like they were bored.

Of course I told them it was because of the kids, which they thought was rather novel. Relieved at how much easier the interview process was than I had imagined, I relaxed.

"Sheesh, I thought you were going to ask if I have a criminal record," I bantered.

They jumped on that. "Oh, do you?"

"No! I don't, but thanks for asking," I answered quickly. "Geez."

I didn't know it then, but those interviews would launch a media blitz. The stories got picked up by other papers through the Associated Press. Then the mainstream press read about our campaign, and they started calling. Before it was all over, the story had even gone international. But, as they say, ignorance is bliss. Having no sense of what a sensation my class and I were creating with my run for Congress, I just focused on what was next. After all these months, I finally knew who I was running against in the primary elections—a casino worker from Vegas named Clay Baty. I couldn't help feeling excited. Democrats in seventeen Nevada counties would be seeing the name of a Reno teacher with no money and no political connections when they went to the polls in the primaries. More than 300,000 people would have the opportunity to vote for me. It was hard to believe.

The next morning I went back to class, filing papers in hand.

"We did it! We're on the ballot!" the kids screamed. Suddenly it was real instead of just being a goal. They thought it was the coolest thing, especially when the different counties began mailing me their sample ballots.

The last month of school was spent wrapping up all the end-of-year projects, which included a big report about the history of war. Each student had selected a different war to study. On parent night, we did a huge presentation with stations and tabletop exhibits. Hors d'oeuvres and beverages were provided for the parents so they could walk around nibbling as if they were at a gallery opening. Each member of my class dressed in the uniform of someone from that time period—like a nurse or a soldier—who had been involved in that war and then spoke in the first person as that character. One girl whose grandfather had fought in World War II dressed up as Adolf Hitler. It was a little disconcerting, but people could walk up and ask questions of a very blond female Hitler. Like the rest of the class, she had become an expert on her topic. When you turn kids loose, they are pretty impressive.

By the last week of school, I could barely handle the knowledge that I would probably never see a large number of these kids again since they'd be moving on to middle school the next year. During the graduation picnic and then the graduation ceremony, I tried to treasure every moment, so I would cement the memory of my students in my mind. I remembered how they'd grown as people, the challenges they had overcome, and the funny or touching incidents that had occurred during the last nine months.

I flashed on comforting Amanda when she'd holed up in the girls' bathroom after her sixth-grade boyfriend, Kyle, had broken up with her. She'd taken off the necklace he'd bought her, thrown it against the wall, and stomped on it as she screamed, "I hate him! I hate him!" By the next week, she had moved on and was fine.

I thought about Brent and Thomas, who had started coming to our homework club to get help after getting zeros for not doing their homework. Since some kids don't have terrific support at home, I ran a study hall an hour a day after school for anyone who wanted to come. Though initially resistant, the two boys finally realized that they just had to dedicate the time and knock out their assignments. Talk about an epiphany!

And Thomas, who hated school and lived for motorcycles, made significant academic strides, passing his classes despite being hospitalized after breaking both arms and legs in a motocross accident and being out of school for months.

Sixth graders go through a tremendous metamorphosis. They come in as little kids and go out as middle schoolers. Inevitably, they go through changes—some traumatic, others less so. Girls often get their periods. Boys can grow four inches taller. And the arrogance that they enter sixth grade with as the big kids on campus dissipates into worry by the end of the year as they anticipate being the little seventh graders on a middle-school campus.

It's always hard to let go of my students after a year of bonding in the classroom. But this year had been even more special. Not a single kid had failed, with a couple actually making it out of special ed. Even Mackenzie, the hardworking, dyslexic daughter of a doctor and a nurse who read at a first-grade level when she started the school year, worked hard and concluded the year as an honor student. A great speaker, she wound up leading committee meetings and even chronicling those meetings in writing. Tall, lanky Stephanie, who was dyslexic as well, also made it out of special ed. Though her mom hadn't consented to her daughter's after-school participation in the campaign, shy Stephanie engaged in our class conversations as much as anybody. I later found out that she made the honor roll the following year in middle school.

We lose many kids because they don't connect with what's being taught or fail to bond with the teacher. That's the problem with teaching to a test, standardized or not. By participating in projects that engaged them intellectually and emotionally, these kids learned to love school and felt as important as they did successful. Perhaps just as significantly, they didn't want to disappoint me. That this connection had lasted the whole year was nothing short of amazing.

Even the good students had blossomed. I was particularly proud of Julie, a cute little thing who had started out the year with very low self-confidence, seeming to want nothing more than to bury herself in a hole. Being a part of that elite club known as the Cahill Campaign gave her something she needed. By the end of the year, she was an outgoing, popular girl with visible self-confidence.

Yes, it was hard to say good-bye to these students, but I knew that every single one of them would march into middle school better equipped to handle what came their way. Win or lose, the campaign had already proved more successful than I could have possibly imagined.

15

Reality Check

★ ★

Now that I was on the ballot, I campaigned harder than ever. Even though I was technically on vacation, I remained in uniform in the khaki pants and campaign T-shirt I wore to school daily. Normally during the four-week break—our year-round school gets three monthlong vacations throughout the year instead of having the whole summer off—I spend the first week in my jammies. It takes a week of sleeping, cooking, doing chores I've put off, or reading a book uninterrupted—and not answering the phone—to depressurize myself. That wasn't an option this year, even though I was so exhausted by the end of school that I wouldn't have made it without the support of colleagues like Todd, who brought Starbucks lattes to keep me going. He knew how dog-tired I was. Todd didn't drink coffee. And he's a Republican, which I teased him about as relentlessly as I do my Republican uncle who is a lobbyist for the Quincy Library Grove (funny name for a lumber lobby) and whom I love dearly.

Comments about my "uniform" ranged from "Oh my

god, I'm so sick of seeing you in that outfit" to "Are you kidding?" But it helped get my name out there and I certainly
couldn't afford most other forms of advertising. So, I was my
own billboard. I'd go to the store, and people would point to
my T-shirt and ask, "Who's that?"

"Oh, it's me," I'd tell them.

"Really, you're running for Congress?"

Inevitably, they'd follow up with questions about my positions on various issues.

As much as I needed the publicity, the attention that my
Cahill for Congress uniform prompted could be unsettling.
I had stopped at an AM/PM gas station to fill my tank when
a teacher from McQueen High School stopped me.

"Where did you get the T-shirt?" he asked with a smile.

"I had it made," I replied.

He looked at me quizzically. "So do you know her?"

"I am her."

His shock quickly gave way to excitement. "Oh, my goodness. It's a pleasure to meet you, Ms. Cahill. I've read about
you and what you're doing. You make our profession proud.
Good job! You've definitely got my support!"

I couldn't help it; I blushed. He was treating me like a
movie star. After thanking him and assuring him that I was
right there in the trenches with him and only too happy to
enlighten the public about our profession, I scrambled into
my car and fled. Planned campaign-related encounters
were much easier to contend with.

I did what I could to maximize my exposure. Kendall
Stagg, who was running for state assembly, continued to ap-
prise me of Democratic-sponsored happenings through
covert e-mails. "Here are the next ten events that I know are
going on," my spy wrote. "Be at this one. That one doesn't
matter. But this one does." Sometimes he supplied me with

specifics. "The AFL-CIO is having a board meeting. Make sure you're there because the unions want to interview you." At other times, he urged me to show up.

"But I'm not invited," I routinely countered.

"Who cares?" he said. "You are a Democratic candidate. You be there."

So I studied the AFL-CIO's issues, and those of the next group and the group after that. Then I appeared at every event I could whether invited or not, and hammered home my educational-funding and middle-class-squeeze messages.

"So many valuable people who could serve our country don't simply because they lack the money to participate. And our country is worse off for it," I preached after warning that if we didn't find a way to retain good teachers, we'd find ourselves in crisis within ten years. And largely because of my students, who believed that if you had campaign material to hand out you would come across as official, I looked as much the part as anyone else. However, we seemed to be the only ones eager to get those leaflets and buttons into the voters' hands.

Shane Piccinini, then-head of the Washoe County Democrats, had assured me that the party would pass out my materials at Democratic events, just as he had assured me that I was on the party's mailing list and would automatically receive notices about upcoming events. But at each campaign event, the handouts or campaign signs from every candidate but me would be displayed and distributed. Though I made sure to get the flyers and yard signs my class and I had created to campaign headquarters, they never seemed to make it to the actual event.

It was hard not to feel like the oversights amounted to intentional slights. "Were you told to ignore me and maybe I'd go away?" I wanted to ask. If that was the plan, it surely backfired. Though I was tentative at first, eventually, the more the party tried to alienate me, the more I wanted to be there. Night after night, I packed Kelton, Kennedy, and O'Keeffe in the car and took them to meetings of the State of Nevada Employees Association, as well as to retirement homes, Democratic clubs, and any other candidate event I could possibly attend. My students often couldn't join me at these evening and weekend events. But my three kids got used to doing their homework or reading a book at the back of the various halls where I spoke, and passing out campaign buttons and leaflets. They also became accustomed to being asked if they were my students. "No, that's our mom," they'd reply, and a funny pause always followed since we don't exactly look alike.

Though I still wasn't good at—and certainly not comfortable with—asking people for their money, frequent speaking engagements had helped me hone other skills. I had gotten pretty good at relating to the electorate I was trying to court, in large measure because I never pretended to be something I wasn't or to know something I didn't. Toward the middle of my June vacation, I was invited to a house party—usually held to support a particular political party, candidate or ballot measure—in wealthy Incline Village.

"What do you think about the 1872 Mining Act?" a gal asked me.

I'd heard of mining acts before, but didn't know any more than that. Since I'm the worst, stuttering liar, I didn't even try to bluff. I looked at her with a blank stare before confessing my ignorance.

She rolled her eyes like I was an idiot. She didn't say a thing, but I knew exactly what was going through her mind. "Oh, god, here's another dumb-ass politician."

"I'm sorry, I don't know what that is, but I'll be happy to

go home and read up on it, and I promise that I will get back to you. I'll e-mail you or call you, whatever you're more comfortable with, and tell you what I think of it."

Her answer, though polite, conveyed her conviction that she would never hear from me.

I looked up the General Mining Act of 1872 as soon as I got home. It turns out that it basically protects foreign and domestic miners from having to pay much in the way of taxes or in compensation for the damage they do to our public lands. Because we're such a huge mining state and the second-largest gold producer in the world, that's a particularly relevant concern in Nevada, where 86 percent of our state is federally owned public property. Mining here has led to some successes, but a lot of mining companies have come through and raped the land. Not only do they deplete our land, but when the price of gold drops or something else changes, they disappear, leaving a god-awful scar on the earth. Somehow the promised land reclamation doesn't materialize.

Gold mining in Nevada isn't like California where there are big nuggets. Here they often bulldoze and dynamite a canyon into the earth. Then they take the dirt and rock, crush it, and dump it in ponds spiked with cyanide, which attaches to microscopic bits of gold. Millions of pounds of rock are pulverized to process each small amount of gold.

Because we're not a very densely populated state, a lot of people think, "Oh, who cares. Nevada is this big wasteland." Well, that's our public land. Besides, each time these small mining towns go boom and bust, the poor people out there working "the industry" are left with nothing. As I write these words, four to five hundred homes are being foreclosed on in Winnemucca because shutting down production is more profitable right now than keeping the mine open. That's as devastating to these small communities as the operation is to the environment.

When I shared my new insights with the woman from Incline who had challenged me, she became one of my biggest fans. I don't necessarily think she suddenly decided I was a great politician or any kind of expert on mining, but my response must have satisfied her. Even better, I had kept my word and provided her with a personal follow-through.

That helped me realize that I didn't need to be so intimidated about talking in front of groups. Confessing that I didn't know something but would get back to the person asking the question was golden. People instantly realized that I wasn't trying to snow them.

Once I had established a bond with the gathering I was addressing, I talked about whatever single topic would most interest that particular group. At Lake Tahoe, I spoke about getting federal dollars to preserve the lake. With seniors, I talked about Social Security, Medicare, and prescription drugs. All you had to do was jump on the group's bandwagon and its members were happy. Eventually, however, I always brought the discussion around to the two issues closest to my heart.

"People always want to blame schools for all our problems. But schools are a mirror of society, and you can see that the village isn't well," I told them. "Yet somehow public schools, which aren't allowed to turn anybody away, are expected to fix it all. They can't begin to do that. They're having enough trouble trying to create the appropriate educational environment for every student, no matter how challenged, that's mandated by law."

Of course, fixing things was one of the reasons I became a teacher. Yes, I was still looking to change the world and our country. I firmly believed that the Horatio Alger myth was just that. How could we spread the message to kids that they can be anything they want to be if they work hard when all too often injustices make that impossible? So I talked about how America is strongest when we have a very large middle class. That's what keeps this country productive and healthy. The rich sometimes seem so wrapped up in protecting themselves and their money that they blame the poor for their own misfortune. It must be easier to sleep at night if you can rationalize that poor people deserve their lot in life because they don't work hard enough. Of course, the poor are simply trying to survive day to day, hoping to have enough to get by, so often they don't have the time or the energy to participate in politics.

"If the middle class keeps shrinking, there goes our country," I said in the many speeches I gave. "If we look back at the 1950s, we had this huge, thriving middle class. No matter what job you picked out of high school, everyone could buy a house and a new car. Your wife was able to stay home. You were able to raise kids, who actually played outside. And you could afford to take your sweetheart to the movies on Friday night and buy dinner and maybe a beer. It's not like that anymore. We are edging people out. I don't know what my poor little guys do who can't make it in the public school system and thanks to state law are denied a diploma because they couldn't pass a test."

People often nodded as I gave voice to their frustrations. I didn't necessarily have a fix-all answer, but I certainly lived the problem and knew how it impacted my family.

Campaigning in Reno gave me a new sense of the city where I've spent most of my life. Reno still has a lot of the Wild West in it, and people still move here for the growth potential and opportunity they sought during the town's mining heyday. Notwithstanding my cynicism about Horatio Alger, rags-to-riches stories aren't merely dreams here. John Ascuaga, the old Basque owner of John Ascuaga's Nugget Casino, started with a small coffee shop. That kind of opportunity can still be found in Reno. Those people who move here to try and fill a niche are tapping into a long history. Reno's exports include Levi's, developed by Levi Strauss and his business partner, Jacob Davis, who in the 1870s invented the copper rivet to secure the pockets of work pants after immigrating to Reno from Germany and Latvia, respectively.

Prospects may have changed since the gold rush, but Renoites haven't lost their ornery sense of independence. A strong libertarian streak means that residents don't like for the government to dictate much of anything, including city ordinances. That may explain the abrupt duality of Reno's unexpected city layout. For starters, the airport is located well within the city borders. It didn't used to be, but sprawling development has taken over the ranch land that used to surround the runways. A nearby feed and tack store just east of the freeway and lush irrigated pastures flanked by brand-new box stores attest to those bygone days.

Horses and cows grazing alongside strip malls aren't the only disparities in a city where urban planning clearly hasn't been a priority. Throughout the city, neighborhoods replete with polished mansions, grounds that look like established parks, and man-made water features large enough to bathe a small family of elephants butt up against new housing tracts that look decidedly lower middle class. No transition. No buffer zone. Few gates. Just a pronounced difference from one side—or one end—of the street to the other.

These days, Reno is pushing up against—and up into— the bare hills around its perimeter. In comparison to the brick structures built in the mid-1800s that define the city's older downtown and residential neighborhoods, the new sand-colored developments blend into the dusty colors of our high desert. The proliferation of these attractively planned developments, however, has cost the city in unexpected ways. Blacktop now covers the wetlands, which served as a natural swamp cooler for the town. Breezes came in off the hills, blew across the watery bird havens, and cooled things down. Now, the heat is absorbed and radiated by the blacktop instead of being dispelled. As a result, Reno's daytime summer temperatures have risen seven degrees over the last thirty years, and we no longer experience that nighttime cooldown typical in high desert communities.

In addition to talking about the impact of development on our environment and our well-being, I also addressed the state's social health problems. It seriously bothers me that Nevada has been called the Mississippi of the West. It ranks in the bottom ten states in many quality-of-life indicators, including high school graduation, teen suicide, teen drug abuse, homicides, child abuse, health insurance coverage, food stamp coverage, and suicide for those over sixty-five. Corporations look at these statistics when deciding to relocate their businesses; despite our highly favorable business tax climate, many don't come because a large percentage of their employees won't relocate to a state with such high-risk statistics for children and families.

The more I learned, the happier I was that I was running. Somebody needed to highlight Nevada's challenges.

16

The Primary Push

★ ★ ★ ★ ★ ★ ★ ★ ★ ★ ★ ★ ★ ★ ★ ★ ★ ★ ★ ★

The primary was fast approaching. Though I technically had four weeks off during June, I spent most of my time campaigning. As always, my last week of vacation was consumed with running off copies, making decorations for the class bulletin boards, creating binders, and generally preparing for the return to school, a fresh pack of kids, and the start of another academic year.

I already knew who my students would be. I had watched them line up outside their classroom and had already greeted a number of them by name. Their teacher, Cathy Linde, had given me a head start by providing notes on every single child leaving her class for mine. "Amazing writer, good vocabulary, excellent speller," read one paragraph. "Mother is a rescuer and needs to let her child become more responsible."

My new students knew me, too. For a year, they had watched the activities of my prior class, knowing that once I got on the ballot, they would have to see me through the primary election, which would be held two months after their return to school in July. Unlike the first time around, not a single mom or dad challenged me or asked that their child not participate.

This crop of kids looked tiny to me compared to the class that had recently graduated to middle school. They were still such babies, scared and nervous that first week. So we went through all the procedural stuff like assigning cubbyholes, how each student gets to be class secretary for a week, where I write homework on the board, and how we turn it in. The training about how to live in our room and how we work things out was summarized in both a student handbook and a parent handbook. All that went home along with a supply list. Then we jumped into the campaign. With the primary just six weeks away, these kids had to fully understand what we were doing and why without a moment's delay.

"I realize a lot of you guys already know this because you're friends with kids who were in my classroom, but I see some new faces, so let's talk about my run for Congress and see where we're at," I told them.

Their excitement about our mission, already high, escalated even more when I added that since their parents had signed off on their participation, they could all become as involved as they wanted in every facet of the campaign.

"Really? Like we could go get interviewed with you?" Nicole asked, clearly more excited about the possibility of getting on television than anything else.

"Of course!" I replied. "Absolutely. I'd love that. I want you to be there."

Cries of "That's cool!" and "Awesome!" filled the room.

They're going to redefine the notion of the media hound, I thought to myself.

"Who wants to be Campaign Manager this week?" I asked. "That means that you'll man the cell phone, take media requests, and schedule interviews through Friday."

Since the position rotated, everybody would eventually have a shot at being the lead dog. So I reviewed protocol with the entire class.

"When people call and want to come talk to us, we can't take away from instructional time, so when could they interrupt us?" I prompted. When the students answered that they could come during PE, recess, or lunch, I added, "So you guys could look at our schedule and book them for those periods. But don't book them during math."

The students trained one another and then monitored one another's phone manner.

"You'd better be careful how you answer, because you never know who's calling us," Ashleigh, a pretty but withdrawn girl who, as the campaign progressed, seemed to come into her own, advised the more rambunctious Sadie as she picked up the phone.

When Michael, a shy but mischievous boy with tremendous artistic talent, or Sam, a phenomenal skier who's much more comfortable flying down a hill than sitting behind a desk, got squirrelly, the others reined them in.

"Hey, no, that's not how it works," said Melissa. "Let me show you."

Since the kids already knew that our instructional time was sacred, they became brutally good at putting people off.

"I'm sorry, but you can't speak with her at this time. She's teaching math right now and can't be interrupted," Melissa said after a reporter asked for me. "How can I help you?"

When the caller insisted on talking to me in person, she

was politely refused. "I'm sorry, that isn't possible. You're going to have to call back at recess or leave a name and number so Ms. Cahill can call you back when she's free."

When I finally did talk to the caller, Melissa's phone manner trumped our interview for the first few minutes.

"That child could work for me!" she exclaimed. "She's amazing!"

"I know," I agreed. "My students are incredibly good at what they do."

The kids knew that their actions could impact the campaign, so they didn't hesitate to check with one another when unsure.

"Wait, what do we do when they say they can't come at PE?" Sadie asked, having put a caller on hold.

"We're supposed to have them talk to Ms. Cahill. Just take down their name and number."

The rule was "Ask three before me," since the knowledge they sought could often be secured within their own group. I wanted them to do as much as possible without me. Kids are disenfranchised from many things, from many grown-up decisions, from many roles. Why not empower them? I had other rules as well, including asking the kids to come up with a suggestion or a solution instead of just coming to me with a problem, and having them propose an alternate assignment if they didn't want to do the one I had asked for.

The new class kicked right into gear, proving that when you set expectations for kids, almost no matter how high, they will meet them. It was such fun to see them become immersed so quickly.

"What's 'filibuster'?" Jordan asked after watching the previous evening's CNN coverage of a bill about to be voted on.

"Does someone want to look it up and report to the whole class?" I asked.

Michael, Robert's heir to the art committee, jumped at the opportunity. Grabbing a dictionary from the bookcase in the reading section, he flipped through the pages until he found the definition. "Filibuster," he read. "Informal term for any attempt to block or delay Senate action on a bill or other matter by debating it at length, by offering numerous procedural motions, or by any other delaying or obstructive actions."

We proceeded to come up with examples and non-examples of filibustering. Inevitably my answers led to more questions, and the discussion kept spiraling until I reminded the students that we had to finish our math. But the campaign took center stage whenever possible.

Since the students needed to immediately gel into a cohesive group of participants who trusted one another, Todd Herman and I started our year with a week at the same Tahoe science camp that had ended our last class. Our hope was that the tight friendships that had formed among the previous year's kids, who suddenly saw one another in a new light, would help us bypass all those months during which they had struggled to learn to appreciate one another. It worked.

Camaraderie and respect blossomed during a week of Tribes activities designed to pose problems to the group that could only be solved through inclusive teamwork. When the kids had to get over a stream using a knotted rope, they had to work together so that no one was left behind. Building sturdy toothpick-and-marshmallow houses, though less of a physical challenge, still demanded creative team strategies and provided lots of laughs. Without having to think much about it, they learned to rely on one another and become a successful team. The knowledge that they were an elite group participating in a superspecial project that no one else was doing also prompted them to bond quickly, which helped since they had to hit the ground—and the campaign trail—running as soon as they started the sixth grade.

Whenever I could, I took kids from my class when I met with groups ranging from retirees to the members of the local synagogue that some hateful person had tried to burn down in 1998. But when Reverend Onie Cooper, an active member of the National Association for the Advancement of Colored People (NAACP) here in Reno, invited me to speak to his congregation at the Baptist church near Traner Middle School, my mother, who was visiting, and my three children came along. (My students didn't join us since it was Sunday.) Upon our arrival at the unassuming church, a tiny old one-story structure, Reverend Cooper brought us right up to a front pew. Other politicians were also in attendance, including Republican candidate for the State legislature Sharron Angle, who some Democrats refer to as "Right Angle." Even so, Reverend Cooper proceeded to introduce me to anyone within reach.

Baptist churches are quite a bit different from the Catholic church that I grew up in. The members of the crowd actively participate, shouting out affirmations and enthusiastic praises. Though I'm certainly not a speaker in the tradition of the church, I did my best.

"Thank you for opening your arms to me and my family," I said. "I share many of the same economic, educational, and environmental concerns that you do. I struggle to keep milk in the fridge, gas in the tank, and nuclear waste out of my backyard! I know what it's like to work hard every day and still be afraid it's not enough. And I worry about what kind of a country this will turn out to be for my three young children. I promise you that should I be sent to Congress, I will not forget these struggles we share, and I will work hard on behalf of all Nevadans to improve our quality of life."

Kelton, Kennedy, and O'Keeffe became a little intimidated when the congregation greeted my short speech with typically interactive enthusiasm.

"Grandma, why do these people keep yelling and shouting things?" Kennedy asked my mom.

Mom suppressed a smile and shushed her, afraid someone might overhear and be offended. Kennedy was even more disconcerted when the woman in her Sunday best seated in the row behind her seemed on the verge of fainting. Reverend Cooper quietly explained to the kids that they didn't need to worry. "She's just moved by the spirit," he said. Instead of being reassured, Kennedy then worried about the spirit touching her. My mother could hardly contain herself as she wiped away tears of laughter.

My schedule had seemed busy up until then though still somewhat manageable. But in August, things went berserk. I probably should have seen it coming. Reno hosts a number of huge events, particularly in the summer. In July, Art Town showcases dancers like Baryshnikov, bands such as The String Cheese Incident, painters, and kids' activities. During Hot August Nights, gorgeous tricked-out vintage cars and their owners take over the town, which goes nuts. Fifty-five hundred cool old cars are officially registered for the event, but another approximately five thousand more show up, along with a couple of hundred thousand car buffs who just want to look. That's the start of nonstop events—which include a motorcycle rally called Street Vibrations, the Air Races, and the Great Balloon Race—that run until October.

My class and I discussed how we should spend our time

campaigning and what events I should attend. The kids pushed for the Rib Cook-Off that every Labor Day weekend takes over downtown Sparks, the town that shares Reno's eastern border. In addition to the barbecue contest, which is all about the pig, big outdoor concerts showcase well-known bands. This year the 1970s multiethnic funk band War was performing for free.

"Ms. Cahill, that's a huge public venue, and we need to be there in our Cahill for Congress T-shirts to hand out buttons and pamphlets because that's a population we should hit," they argued.

"Okay," I agreed. "Sounds good to me."

We set up in Victorian Square, a big open area close to the temporary concert stage and alongside the street vendors and arts-and-crafts tents. Already acting like seasoned pros, the kids went to work.

"Please vote for Ms. Cahill. She's running for Congress. She's our teacher."

"What? Are you helping her?"

"Yes, we're helping her. We're running her campaign."

People chuckled and asked questions, clearly astounded by these engaging little people who at the age of eleven and twelve clearly knew how to handle themselves.

When Ashleigh and Michael approached an old hippie who was obviously enjoying the music from his younger days, he couldn't contain his amazement.

"Whoa, man, I haven't seen kids in the political scene like this since the sixties."

That cracked them up.

"Would you like a button?" Ashleigh asked, still laughing.

"Right on," the man answered, pinning the button on his T-shirt. "Awesome."

Even though I told my students that they had to stay together in groups of threes, I didn't let them get very far from me. Nervous to be in such a crowded venue with kids, I wanted to make sure no one disappeared or got into trouble. Still, before long I noticed an increasing number of people wearing our buttons. What a kick in the pants!

The events kept coming. Despite having moved on to seventh grade, ten of last year's students—the core crew—often turned out to help. A number of my current students' parents also lent a hand, copying and collating campaign materials for us since we couldn't afford to print them on glossy cardstock, carpooling kids to events, and carrying boxes heavy with buttons.

While the campaign venues changed, my basic message remained the same. I told voters what I was about and asked for their support. I knew they wouldn't promise me an endorsement no matter how much they liked me. You have to make it through the primary first. Until then, no one wants to contribute to your campaign or come out too strongly in favor of your candidacy because they don't want to burn any bridges in case you don't win. So they'll say things like, "I'm certainly with the Democrats, but a number of these candidates are my friends, so I'm going to abstain from coming out too strongly for any of them." That's really frustrating when you're trying to survive during this period.

Though I had gotten wind that my only opponent for the primary—the casino worker from Vegas who I would have been happy to vote for—wasn't running very hard, I didn't let myself think about what that could mean. For one thing, I figured that since he came from Vegas and the population down there is so big, he would be a shoo-in. Besides, despite my ferocious campaigning, the notion of my being the Democratic candidate for Congress still seemed far-fetched.

Before I knew it, the primary elections were upon us. Since we had spent a lot of time talking about the primary process, my class already understood concepts that many adults surprisingly don't. My mother still makes wild comments like, "Well, it's too bad I can't vote in a Republican primary, because I would love to vote against that rat bastard to make sure he doesn't get the nod."

"That's exactly why they don't let you vote in a primary for a party you don't belong to, Mom," I answer. "Each party has the right to choose its own candidates."

Now, my mother *does* know this, but she still dreams of being able to meddle in Republican affairs. She's quite entertaining when she really gets on a roll.

On September 5, 2000, the day of the primary, I gave a brief classroom speech about how well the class had worked together and how much they had accomplished in such a short period of time. Then, with cries of "Good luck!" echoing in my head, I went off to vote. I stepped into the voting booth as if in a surrealistic dream and pulled the curtain. Looking down, I saw my name on the ballot. My name! Wishing my students from both classes could be crammed in there with me, I carefully voted for myself.

The following morning, I woke up, threw on my robe, grabbed a cup of coffee and went out to get my newspaper, my hair still a big moppy mess and smeared residues of makeup on my face. Anxious to see how a number of primary elections had turned out, I plopped down and opened the paper. My usual excitement at seeing who had made it through was tinged with nervousness. *What if my opponent had walked away with the election?* I thought. *I'd be done.* I realized that despite the hardships, stopping the campaign would be a huge disappointment. I had finally gotten used to running and actually enjoyed it now.

The front page trumpeted the Senate race results. I had to open to page three or four and look through all the other races before I found the 2nd Congressional District results. Jim Gibbons would be the Republican candidate, which figured, since as a popular incumbent he had not faced a challenge from inside his party. And *I* would be his Democratic opponent.

Holy cow! This isn't over, I thought, more stunned than anything else. *I am going to the final dance.*

17

Public Opinions

★ ★ ★ ★ ★ ★ ★ ★ ★ ★ ★ ★ ★ ★ ★ ★ ★ ★

I hadn't anticipated ever knowing a taste of winning when it came to politics. I let myself savor the win even as a slight sense of terror about the real battle ahead tinged my victory party of one. *Okay, Reps and Dems,* I thought. *We're going head-to-head now.*

Derrick, the man supposedly closest to me, greeted news of my triumph with a dismissive "You got lucky." No acknowledgment of how hard I had worked. No acknowledgment that with no money and no connections, I hadn't just gotten my name on the ballot, I had won! As usual, his lack of support only subsided when the media or party big shots were around. Then he'd smile for the camera and try to weasel his way into the conversation. By then I was so used to his ways that his reaction barely fazed me. I knew better than to hope for support from him.

That morning, as always, the kids dumped their backpacks in a massive pile by the classroom door and scampered off to play outside. When the bell rang, they ran over to find their stuff and gather in a mob of a line. I was less strict about that than other teachers, like Miss Zellerman, who insisted that her students form a perfectly straight line every time. I figured I had a lot more to worry about than kids lining up in a haphazard zigzag formation.

As the students filed into the classroom, I greeted them one by one as I did every morning, bantering with them as they got their books and the rest of their things put away.

"Hi, pumpkin!" I said to Nicole, a fiery little girl who will probably be on the Nevada ballot herself one day. "Did you win your game last night?"

"Ms. Cahill, you won the primary," she shot back.

I smiled. "I know. *We* won!" I said, delighted that she had followed the election results on her own even though I hadn't assigned that as homework. "We'll talk about that later when we meet as a class."

The kids cheered the news of our victory. My previous class had gotten me on the ballot; this class had helped me win the primary. The presidential contest between Al Gore and George W. Bush made the fact that we would be able to participate through the entire election process—rather than just the primary—even more exciting.

"We're not done yet. We get to keep going," I told them. "This is awesome. How much fun are we going to have?"

I had no clue how winning the primary would impact my life.

Now that our campaign had shifted from the primary to the general election, we needed to come up with a new plan.

"What do we do now?" I asked my class.

"Can't we find some dirt on Gibbons?" a couple of the kids asked.

"No, we're not doing that. If you're running a marathon, you don't want to trip everyone around you. It's about winning on your own merits."

I had signed an oath saying that I wouldn't do any negative campaigning, and unlike most candidates today, I took that seriously. So our plan revolved not around competing with my opponent, Jim Gibbons, but rather doing our best and presenting ourselves in the most effective way.

Still, I was concerned about parental reaction. This new batch of parents had all received the same disclaimer I had sent out the prior year, indicating that participation would be voluntary and ungraded, and that the campaign wasn't about positions, but rather about the process. But in the fall of 1999, I had been running to run. Once I got the party's nomination, I couldn't avoid questions about my positions on various controversial issues. Though I still didn't stress those points in the campaign and I didn't discuss them with children, I wasn't going to dodge them if asked by adults or the press. The voters deserved to know what I thought.

I especially worried about those parents I knew to be religious, right-wing Republicans. For starters, they would clearly be pro-life while I was pro-choice. The fact that I didn't support carte blanche abortion when it came to minors would cost me a perfect score with Planned Parenthood, but I'm sure it didn't make my stance any more palatable to those parents who wholeheartedly disagreed with me about the issue in general. Still, not one complained, even though my commitment not to discuss the issues now stopped at the classroom door.

A media free-for-all started that same day, with local newspapers and television news stations wanting to know about me—the Democratic candidate—and what my run for Congress was all about. The fact that sixth graders were handling my campaign launched my students straight into the spotlight as well.

In addition to print and television journalists grilling me on my positions, every lobbying group you could imagine—including ones I'd never even heard of—came out of the woodwork. It was open season. I was inundated with policy materials, along with questionnaires about my positions. If the groups liked what I said, they endorsed me. Their endorsement meant not only potential votes, but also potential contributions. Considering that the campaign bank account contained a mere couple hundred dollars, that would help. But first I had to convince them that I was worthy of their financial support—and even more important, their endorsement—by filling out stacks of opinion papers. When organized lobbying groups like the American Association of Retired Persons (AARP) sent out cards that listed their endorsed candidates and said, "Please vote this way," I wanted them to say "Please vote for Tierney Cahill." And the only way for that to happen was for me to answer those questionnaires and write those position papers.

"How am I going to get this done?" I wondered, completely overwhelmed.

Most candidates have a staff to handle these kinds of things. My staff, by definition, couldn't even be involved. So I was on my own. I read the stacks of literature from the dozens and dozens of organizations, answered the questionnaires, and wrote position papers as honestly as I could on topics ranging from Medicaid and Social Security for the AARP to birth control for the Population Institute. Whether I was writing responses to the National Organization for Women (NOW), to right-wing organizations like the Eagle Forum that I knew I would never see eye-to-eye with, or to groups I had never even heard of, I answered each with the same seriousness. Every response took hours of research, as I had to look at what was going on, read as much as I could online, figure out the party's stance on the issue, and then come up with my own viewpoint. Some organizations only cared about a couple of issues, so those were easier to deal with. Others had multiple concerns, which they tried to spin in different ways to draw out your true colors.

This is like being in college again, I thought as I wrote unending papers outlining and defending my beliefs in the wee hours of the morning when I would much rather have been sleeping. I didn't confer with anyone about whether my answers were politically in line or offensive. I didn't even think about whether my answers would prompt the organization to score me high or low. I just followed my own conscience.

Even though I'm a Democrat, for example, I think I scored okay with the National Rifle Association (NRA) because I wasn't antigun. My dad hunted, so I grew up around guns. On the other hand, Jim Gibbons probably had a perfect NRA score. He's a smart politician who has taken pictures in full-on hunting gear to show that he's a Nevada boy. Can't blame him there; that's just good campaigning. But as a teacher who sees the stress among our administrators, teachers, and students every time there's another school shooting, I am concerned about the access minors have to weapons. I believe that criminals and the mentally ill shouldn't be allowed to purchase guns. Safety locks also seem like a pretty logical proposition to me, as does locking up one's guns at home. That's certainly what we do in my home.

Then there's the ammunition. I talked to the local sheriff's department about police vest–piercing bullets. "Why do we need them?" I asked. Not surprisingly, law enforcement doesn't feel real good about those either.

During these personal interviews, I tried to find a connection to give me the insider's perspective.

"Hey, will you take me on a tour of the county jail?" I asked Bill Ames, a deputy I had gotten to know who happened to be president of the Washoe County Sheriff's Deputies Association and who has become a dear friend. "I'd like to see the conditions that deputies have to work under."

He loved me for that. "You're one of the few frickin' candidates who would even spend time down here in a jail," he told me.

I knew of the long hours and overcrowded jails. But I needed to see for myself.

"Well, I want to understand what it is you guys have to do and what you're facing. I've heard stories about feces being thrown on officers, along with other activities that expose them to blood-borne hepatitis."

My visit to the jail, along with the ride-along I had also requested, didn't just set me apart from the other candidates who hadn't done either. It allowed me to win over union representatives through casual one-on-one conversations, rather than being in a formal hot seat.

Candidates always try to make themselves seem down-to-earth and affiliated with various groups, but often those ties are made of dental floss. Certainly you can't belong to everything, but you can connect with those groups that you belong to as well as with those you don't. Those human bonds are the most valuable.

Some attempts to connect went less well. Since casinos are the wheel that turns the state, I met with a couple of casino owners and an interesting character named Ferenc Szony, who runs the Sands Hotel Casino here in town. Over coffee, he went on a rampage about unions.

"I hate them, hate them," he raged as I bit my union tongue.

He told me about the painters who hung their banner, which read "Local 167 Painter's Union," on his seventeen-story-high building as they worked.

"You either take that banner down or get off my job site!" he screamed.

"But we always hang our banner so people know who's doing the job."

"I will not do any of that propaganda crap to support your stinking union. I'll go hire nonunion on purpose if you don't take that down."

I just sat there and listened to his whole speech. *Wow, we really aren't going to have much in common,* I thought. *Okay, well, I know what not to talk about with him.* I was very glad that I had never had to work for this "I'll-fire-your-ass-if-you-don't-do-what-I-tell-you" guy. I could have if the timing had been different. Ironically, the first real job I had—if you don't count a two-week stint at McDonald's—was working for a summer as a hostess at one of the restaurants in The Sands before he managed it. I was sixteen.

I didn't get any money from him, which didn't surprise me. After that whole conversation, I was sure he hated Democrats, and that was fine. I also didn't get any money from the construction industry guy who I'd been warned was a "complete lecher."

"If you're going to see him, make sure you wear a skirt where he can see your calves, and it wouldn't hurt to wear a low-cut blouse either," I was advised.

Eew! I thought. Needless to say, I refused to dress the part. Still, his lack of financial support took me aback since I had been a part-time real estate agent for years on the weekends and supported many of the issues the construction industry faced.

As careful as I was to keep policy out of the classroom, I couldn't control what students saw in the press and brought up in class. That month, a lobbyist asked me what I thought about my opponent, Jim Gibbons, sponsoring a bill to extend the patent for Claritin, which basically meant that the pharmaceutical company Schering-Plough would hold the corner on that market and that nobody else could make a similar drug.

"The Congressman is working to extend Claritin's patent so that this pharmaceutical company can continue to make millions of dollars on a drug that's falsely inflated in price, and that millions of people afflicted with allergies and asthma need and can't afford," the lobbyist argued. "Don't you think it's odd that he's backing that?"

I did. All three of my own children have asthma, and I knew firsthand what it was like not to be able to afford their medication. *How is it the order of business in Congress to extend patents for private companies to make more profits?* I wondered. To me this seemed so inappropriate and downright wrong that I wrote a media release with the lobbyist's help and sent it to the press.

Up until then, Gibbons had not responded once to our campaign. I'm sure his advisors said, "Jesus, Mary, and Joseph, please don't say anything about this teacher because the world thinks she's an angel right now and you're going to look like an ogre if you say anything negative about her."

This time the press cornered the Congressman and he had to respond. "Unfortunately, I think Ms. Cahill is misinformed on this topic and has not done her homework," he told reporters. "But she's a very talented teacher and I admire her for what she's doing."

That was the end of any press coverage about the bill, which was never passed.

My students, however, were beside themselves about the exchange.

"He finally responded to something!" they crowed, elated not just by the acknowledgment that we existed, but also by the kudos about me.

His gentle response was surely politically motivated. But while a campaign spearheaded by students made it very hard for people to attack me, it became a double-edged sword, because it was also hard to get anyone to discuss the issues.

"I am a serious candidate!" I wanted to say.

But it was hard to get the press to focus on much more than how cute our campaign was. And cuteness was not going to win the race.

18

Nonstop

★ ★ ★ ★ ★ ★ ★ ★ ★ ★ ★ ★ ★ ★ ★ ★ ★ ★ ★ ★

I have a tendency to take on too much.

"You are absolutely not allowed to say 'yes' to one more thing," my principal ordered a couple of years ago when in addition to teaching full-time, cocktailing part-time, and selling real estate on the weekends, I was running the student store; coaching volleyball, middle-school basketball, high school basketball, and high school softball; working as an eighth-grade advisor; and functioning as the National Education Association (NEA) union rep. "This is insane. How can you do the work of four people and be a single mom? You're going to kill yourself."

"I don't know, I just do it," I answered.

"Tierney, do you ever not operate at high speed?"

"Oh, no, not really," I answered. "I just don't know what to do with downtime, so I fill it."

By the end of the Cahill for Congress 2000 campaign, however, I could have killed for some of that downtime.

I was teaching forty hours a week and waiting tables several nights a week. The other nights I attended multiple campaign events, sometimes hitting two to three dinners to show my smiling face. On the weeks that the kids were with their dad, I really went on a full-out blitz because I knew I didn't have to worry about getting them to bed. So if I had to be somewhere until 11 o'clock at night that was no big deal. I suffered, but at least they didn't.

Once I finally got home, having already been running nonstop, I still had papers to grade and an ever-increasing flood of correspondence to contend with. I answered every e-mail myself. I answered every letter. I answered every single phone call. That alone was hugely time-consuming and exhausting, but who else was going to do it? How could I not respond to someone who had sent me a $20 check? That would have been rude.

When the opinion papers hit, I really thought I was running as hard as I could. I was wrong. Now that I was The Democratic Candidate, the demands on me continued to skyrocket as organization after organization demanded that I meet with them in person. Democratic core groups from the NAACP and Hispanic organizations to women's groups and unions all expected me to make time for them. "Congratulations, you won your primary and we're hoping to see you at our meet-the-candidate dinner as the Democratic candidate for Congress," some wrote. Others were less subtle. "Our voice must be heard. You need to learn firsthand about our issues."

Oh my god, I thought. I had little time for my family as it was. But the election was just two months away, and funding was at the top of the priority list. That meant more meet and greets. Even the teacher's union required a song and dance before it ponied up. Having been an NEA member for eight years, I figured it would simply hand me its support. Nope. In fact, the head lobbyist at the Nevada

State Education Association (NSEA), whose name funnily enough is Debbie Cahill, challenged me the first time I called.

"Are you even a member?" she asked. "I've never heard of you."

Am I a member!? I've since grown to really like Debbie, but that pissed me off. Sitting in my car talking on my cell phone, I opened my wallet, fished out my union card, and read off my member number, each numeral firing through my teeth like a bullet.

"Why don't you try looking this up?" I growled. "I've been a member since the first day I became a public schoolteacher."

I paid union dues every month. I didn't necessarily expect her to know who I was, but why assume that I wasn't a member? I'd hoped for a more welcoming introduction over the phone.

Once she verified that I had indeed been a member for almost a decade, I was invited to speak to the executive board. But instead of being warm and fuzzy, the union's local, state, and national representatives drilled me to the point that I got surly with them.

"You know what? I expect you to support me," I announced. "I am the only candidate in the classroom. I am the only one who knows your issues. I am only one who knows how these things are impacting kids. All these other people can spout their philosophies, but I am living what you all preach. I am doing it. I am there. I am on the front lines."

Then they asked me whether I supported Social Security and whether I thought that everyone should have to pay into it.

"Yes," I said, unaware that I was totally blowing it. "I support Social Security. My poor grandparents worked their whole lives, and that's all they had to survive on while they took care of many others. They did their part. My grandpa served in World War II. My grandma worked like Rosie the Riveter, building airplanes in warehouses. So absolutely. I think we owe our aging Americans a way to not live in poor-houses or be homeless."

One of the local higher-up lobbyists, Elaine Lancaster, a neat gal and tough old broad, pulled me into the hallway.

"What?" I asked in a huff. "I do believe that people de-serve Social Security."

Worried because the board would be voting on whether to support my candidacy, she gave me what amounted to a finger-wagging lecture.

"Listen, kid, that's not the point," she said, wasting no time on niceties. "I understand why you said what you said, because my parents also survived on Social Security. But here's the game, honey. We teachers don't pay Social Secu-rity. We get state retirement. So why would you want to pay into Social Security if you don't get it?"

"Oh, okay," I answered. "Didn't know that one. Sorry."

"That's all right. I think you're going to be okay. You hit it out of the ballpark telling them that you expect their sup-port. Good for you."

Huh! I thought.

The board called me back in and said it was going to back me. It ended up giving me $1,000, one of the largest amounts I received from an organized group.

I got $100 from the WUF Pack and hardly did a thing. It checked out my positions on the Cahill for Congress web-site, sent me a short questionnaire, and then mailed me a check. "We're endorsing you because you are a young fe-male, and we want more young females to be involved in this political regime," announced the pack of educated female executives. Since their acronym stood for their main criterion—Women Under Forty—I certainly qualified.

The campaign suddenly exploded like a balloon filled with confetti when Democratic clubs way out on the east side of Nevada made it clear that they expected me to be at every event they were throwing. Travel and appearances across the state escalated as I jumped back and forth between Carson City and small farm towns. Congressional District 2 is one of the largest in the nation. With the exception of downtown Las Vegas, it covers all of Nevada, geographically the seventh-largest state in the nation, behind Alaska, Texas, California, Florida, Montana, and Arizona. That's quite a lot of ground to cover, and I truly did not have the funds to travel to all of our "cow counties." But I quickly learned that if I didn't make an appearance at these functions, no matter how small or how far away, the participants just talked trash about me for snubbing them. So I did my best to get there, unless logistics made attendance either impossible or ineffective.

Timing proved an even more difficult issue to work around. "We're having this breakfast and you need to be here," organizers would say.

That always cracked me up.

"Do any of you folks have jobs?" I asked each time. " 'Cause I work every day. How do you work and still manage to attend a function at ten in the morning?"

The way our political system is structured, you must be an elitist to participate. How can you get in the game when you are expected to give speeches during a workday?

Whether I saw them personally or not, each group made it clear that this wasn't just a school project—people in this state were counting on me. Until then, I had known that I was "the" candidate, but it was still a class project, right?

Not so much, I suddenly realized. My responsibility no longer lay just with my class or the individuals who had supported my campaign.

For too long Republicans had ignored many groups, especially the disenfranchised. Northern Nevada was a safe haven for Republicans, which meant that a lot of people were desperately looking for me to speak for them. I had to honor that. My own financial struggle made me think about all the people in this country who didn't have the benefit of the education I had received and who hadn't had the opportunities I had. What happened to them? I owed it to all Nevadans to try my best to win.

19

Too Much

★ ★ ★ ★ ★ ★ ★ ★ ★ ★ ★ ★ ★ ★ ★ ★ ★ ★ ★

Despite being stretched so thin in so many ways, I couldn't deny that my life had become downright exhilarating. People say that once you run for office, you'll catch the bug and want to do it again. I totally felt that. The romance of campaigning, along with the fascinating people I was meeting and the sense of being a player, was addictive. Instead of just reading about city council meetings and the like in the newspaper, I had become a part of the discussion. And when the press, organization members, and voters questioned me, I could steer the conversation toward education issues such as vouchers, which I feel are unfair, or environmental issues like Yucca Mountain, where the federal government has threatened to store nuclear waste. As a candidate, I was able to have a voice and maybe help shape the dialogue. But that sense of intoxication couldn't make up for day after day of missed time with my children and night after night of missed sleep.

"You know, the kids haven't seen you. You're tired. You're running yourself ragged," my ex-husband, Lamont, who's still one of my closest friends, chided. "Look at you. You're worn out."

He was right. On an afternoon when I finally managed to squeeze in one of Kennedy's softball games, I remained in the car to watch from the outfield as I answered calls and letters. I had been able to attend so few games over the last year that this one took on special importance. Despite my best efforts, however, I fell asleep, too spent to stay awake a second longer.

"Mom, did you even see my hit?" Kennedy demanded, her irritable knock on the car window waking me up once the game was over.

"Yes, of course I did," I lied. "That was awesome!"

Horrible motherly guilt wedged itself even deeper into my psyche. That should have been my clue that I just couldn't do it all.

When things get tough, the tough get going. At least that's what they say. But I had no idea how I was going to pay the stack of bills in front of me. Over the summer, the two owners of the restaurant I worked in three nights a week had asked if I could come in to talk to them.

"This isn't working out," they told me.

"What do you mean?"

"We need you to be available to work forty hours a week."

I just looked at them. I had been forced to juggle times and shifts lately, but I had never worked forty hours a week. How could I as a teacher?

"I've always been part-time," I said.

"Well, we're changing that. We want people who can commit that kind of time."

Doubting the truth of that response but with no way to counter, I collected my last check and was done. In some ways, I was relieved to no longer be waiting tables until two or three in the morning, especially since I was already putting in those kinds of hours on the campaign. It's really hard to get to bed at that atrocious hour night after night and then try to be normal the next day. But how would I find another source of income?

My third job, real estate, was unpredictable at best. I could go six months without ever having a property to buy or sell. Luckily, after a long dry spell, a very dear friend I taught with and her husband were having me show them houses. We had known each other for nearly twenty years, since attending Reno High together. Over the years as their Realtor, I had helped them sell two homes and buy one. Now they were ready to purchase another, which would be one of the most expensive homes I had been involved with. The commission—3 percent of half a million—would help out a lot. I'd only get 70 percent of that, since my broker takes his cut. Still, ten thousand dollars is a huge chunk of money.

I had shown them properties all summer and into the fall, but they were very particular. Since they had moved in with family, however, they didn't feel pressed. "We don't mind waiting because we don't want to buy just anything," my friend assured me. "We want to find the one we want."

Then she left me a message on my cell phone.

"You know, I feel terrible saying this, but I bought a house today," she said. "The Realtor at the open house said he could write the offer and I knew you were at school, so I went ahead and just had him do that. But I feel really good that you were able to sell our other house. I'm glad we were able to help you."

I was devastated. Her mother had been a Realtor, so she knew better than to have someone show her homes for four months and then walk into an open house and buy from the

Realtor there. She also knew how hard things were for us. One year she had even thrown a birthday party for my daughter because I was too broke to do it. Her betrayal was as shocking as it was hurtful.

God, how do you do that to a friend? I thought. I had been so hopeful that things were finally going to get better for my children and me. Instead, they got worse.

As much as I knew that Derrick was basically another bad choice I'd made, I couldn't help feeling angry that he hadn't bought into the "Okay-let's-all-be-a-family" notion. Just moving in together could have lightened the load. I didn't want to live with someone so dysfunctional, but I was desperate to ease our financial crisis.

I even wondered from time to time whether the kids wouldn't be better off with their father. It seemed so unfair to have to say, "Sorry, we don't have any milk." I could live on Top Ramen, but that wasn't right for kids, and it bothered me that I couldn't do better for them. If Lamont took them for a while, I could downscale to a studio apartment and save money.

As it was, the outflow just never seemed to end. Whether it was $50 to sign up for baseball, new shoes, or picture day, it had always been hard to keep up with the expenses. Now it was impossible. The kids learned to scrounge in the car for change. That, along with the anonymous gift certificates to Winco Foods, helped us through more than once. But that was when I still had part-time work. Now instead of making extra money, I was spending it.

Campaign expenses, like extra gas, fees, and additional car upkeep, were killing me. Every drive to Carson City or Douglas County meant that I had to fill the tank. Thirty dollars doesn't seem like much, but when you're not sure if you can buy milk, it matters. The gas could have been cov-

ered by campaign donations, but I was uncomfortable using money in any way that seemed personal. I had inves-
tigated whether the new clothes I had to purchase for
campaign appearances were covered, only to find out that
they weren't.

My inexperience probably made me overly cautious, but
I worried about inadvertently crossing any lines—especially
since they seemed so arbitrary. But there was nothing sub-
jective about the state of my finances. During my last campaign appearance, I had stood with my back to the wall
as much as possible to hide the run in my panty hose. I
couldn't afford $3.50 for another pair—that represented a
gallon of milk. The event had cost $30 to join the group and
another $30 for the rubber-chicken dinner I barely got to
eat. I wanted to stuff the rolls in my purse and take them
home. I could have used them for sandwiches.

In full throttle on the campaign, with no time to even
think about replacing the income we had lost, "bohemian
dinners" became all too common.

"Bohemia?" the kids asked. "Where's that?"

"Oh, it's in Europe—very swanky place. So let's eat Bohemian."

Then I pulled out whatever I could find in the cupboard.
"Okay, we've got pita bread. What else do we have? We have
green beans. Good. And peanut butter."

We managed to make it through. When I came home to
find that the power had been cut, we got out the candles
and pretended we were camping. The next day I scrounged
up enough money to have it turned back on. But the struggle quickly got old.

Now I readied myself for an all-too-familiar juggling act.

"Which bills am I not going to pay this month?" I wondered as I looked down at the kitchen table.

I knew I could skip a month on my college loan payment and on the capital gains taxes I owed even though my ex-husband and I made almost nothing on the sale of the house we had shared. But when I added up the bills I was really going to *have* to pay—like rent and electricity—I wasn't going to have enough for gas, groceries, or anything else. I could pay the essential bills, but then we would have nothing to live on.

I had been in this position way too many times since the campaign had started.

This is not *what I signed up for!* I thought, the thrill of running taking a backseat to the strain. *This is so outrageous and I'm so tired,* I argued with myself. *Look what this is doing to me. Look how this is impacting my family. This isn't what I got into the campaign for. I need to just quit.*

The internal contention was not new. Neither was the retort.

You cannot quit! You cannot! What message does that send? When things get hard, do you quit? No!

But I was just doing this to prove a point. This whole running-for-Congress thing was just supposed to be a class project, I argued back. *Had I known what I was in for, I never would have agreed to do it.*

There were just eight more weeks to go. After a year of effort and people relying on me to be their voice, I couldn't back out just because things were tough. Neither could I tell anyone how destitute I was. That news flash would discredit my campaign. More important, I didn't want my family to realize that I wasn't making it. And I could never, ever allow my money problems to be known at school. Teachers are supposed to be role models. They have the pencils when you don't. They have the paper when you don't. Who buys all that? The teacher. And when you've forgotten your lunch money, who do you turn to? The teacher.

This teacher, however, didn't have it to give. I was exhausted trying to save face on so many fronts. And I was angry as hell.

I had done everything right. Your parents tell you that if you go to college, live an honorable life, work hard, and play by the rules, things will be okay. But they weren't. I had been a good wife and a good mother, and yet now I was divorced. I had earned my degree and become a respected teacher, and yet couldn't support my family on my salary. Having taken on extra jobs, I worked harder than I should have to without ever getting a break, and still there wasn't enough money. Just one paycheck away from being homeless, I had even gone to check out the day-by-day motels above the railroad tracks and the Truckee River that house transients. I actually found one where the four of us could squeeze into a single room should we get to that point. But the visit disgusted and mortified me.

Oh my god, I can't sink this low, I thought.

My children had figured out long ago that things were tight because of my career choice.

"So when you grow up, do you want to be teacher like your mommy?" Kennedy's kindergarten teacher asked her a couple of years before the campaign started.

"No way!" my five-year-old daughter answered without a moment's hesitation. "They don't make any money! Are you kidding? I would never be a teacher!"

"Mommy, you never have any money. How come you keep doing this?" my children asked from time to time. I felt bad when they questioned why I stayed in teaching, but I felt even worse when they stopped requesting things like clothes or school supplies. That they had obviously been programmed by answers like "No, we just don't have the money" made me feel guiltier than not being able to provide for them.

Still, I loved teaching. My career was not negotiable, even if I did have to supplement it with part-time work. But as things got increasingly desperate, the Cahill for Congress campaign seemed positively disposable. I looked down at the pile of bills I couldn't pay and felt completely depleted.

I'm killing myself, killing my kids, I thought. *We're so broke. Short of Jim Gibbons being caught in a compromising position with a Boy Scout, there's no way I can win this race. This is insane.*

The circumstances of my life, along with the anger and frustration I'd held inside for so long, threatened to overwhelm me. In the past I would cry or punch my pillow and scream. Then I'd just keep going. It wasn't like I had a choice then and I didn't have one now. I couldn't just throw myself on the ground and scream "I'm done!" because the kids would still show up in my bedroom the following morning looking for breakfast, my students would still come to class looking for an engaged teacher, and the voters would still expect me to fulfill my obligations as the Democratic candidate. Like breathing, I just had to proceed without thinking about it too much, which is exactly what I had done for the last year. But the weight of everything had become so unbearable that I couldn't fake it anymore.

I had to talk to someone to cleanse myself of the burdens that were dragging me down. Anyone. But I couldn't be drop-dead honest with a single person I knew. I couldn't even talk to my best friend, Stacey. Admitting that you're flat-ass broke isn't just awful, it's almost like asking for help. And I wasn't about to do that.

As the bands of self-control that I always cinched so

tightly started to loosen, I began to bawl uncontrollably. Reluctantly, with shame and not a little self-loathing for displaying such weakness, I picked up the phone and slowly dialed the number of a local suicide hotline. Fearful of being identified, I refused to share even my first name. But boy did I unleash. Finally, the person on the other end of the line asked me if I had plans to hurt myself or others.

"No!" I exclaimed, deeply offended at the suggestion. Imagine . . . a suicide hotline operator thinking that you might want to harm yourself.

"Then why are you calling?" she asked, clearly confused.

"I just needed an anonymous person to vent to."

I was mad at the world. When personal loans from my principal and the vice principal who I thought hated me helped me pay the power and day-care bills, I had to add humiliation to the mix.

That same week, as I was tucking O'Keeffe into bed, he said, "You know I was thinking about this, and if you win, you're going to Washington, D.C., right?"

"Right," I answered. In my heart, I knew I wasn't going to win, but I could never say that out loud. If you have advanced cancer, you don't say you're going to die. There are things you don't put voice to.

"So you're going to miss all my baseball games, right?"

O'Keeffe lived for T-ball. To this day, all he wants to do is play baseball. Caught off guard, I said, "Uhhhh, I don't know. I'll probably miss a lot of them."

"That's okay, because I know you'll be doing it to help a lot of people and that's more important to me than my games."

Exhausted and overwhelmed by his unselfishness, I went into my room and cried silently as the house quieted to the lull of children sleeping peacefully.

20

It's Up to Me

* *

My seven-year-old son had snapped me back to where I needed to be. With a renewed sense of resolve and just a week before we went on break, I talked to the class about how we could best utilize our time off.

"We only have six weeks to the election, and we haven't walked any precincts yet," I told them. "I'm running for the entire state of Nevada, so there's no way to get to every house or even every neighborhood or county. But I still believe that it's important to go door-to-door."

When a number of students agreed to walk the precincts with me, we decided that we needed to create a flyer to hand out.

"We don't think it's right to say, 'Vote for our teacher,' " Nicole announced.

"So what's our goal here?" I asked.

"Well, we really just want people to be involved. We want people to go vote. But if they don't know who they want to vote for, we could ask them to vote for you."

"Well, okay, that's fine with me, I guess," I answered. "And if they want to ask me questions they can."

"Oh, yeah, we should tell them that too. They can call you."

As with every other piece of campaign literature we created, they referred voters to me by giving out my phone number. That was probably hugely foolish of me, but how do you run for public office as the voice of the public and not be accessible? That doesn't make sense to me.

The final letter presented my class's sense of priorities clearly and succinctly:

Dear Neighbor:

We are out today walking your neighborhood to encourage the citizens of this great state to vote on November 7. We are too young to vote (ten to twelve years old), but we realize the importance of participating in our democracy in order for our country to stay healthy. We don't particularly care who you vote for, just that you vote.

Our teacher, Ms. Tierney Cahill, has agreed to run for Congress to prove to us that anyone can participate in the political process. We have been running her campaign. We have all learned a great deal, Ms. Cahill included! Our main goal is to one day participate in the political process ourselves by voting and maybe even becoming a public servant. We don't want to tell you who to vote for, but if you're undecided, we encourage you to learn about the candidates and vote your values. If you are still undecided, we would appreciate you considering Ms. Cahill for the office of House Representative, District 2. Just in case you're unsure where District 2 is, it covers all of Nevada except for metropolitan Clark County.

Ms. Cahill is willing to answer any questions you may have. Feel free to call her at our campaign headquarters [which was my house] at 323-1186.

Thank you for your time and thank you for voting!!!

Sincerely yours,
Ms. Tierney Cahill's Students

The letter, a simple xerox on white paper, was signed by whoever was walking the precincts on the days it was handed out. We also stapled our business/campaign card, with the logo the kids had designed, to the top.

Nine boys and girls, about a third of the class, arrived at my place the next morning and quickly put on their campaign T-shirts over their nice outfits. My three children were already dressed in their Cahill for Congress best and anxious to get started.

Before heading out, we analyzed the city, evaluating neighborhoods to target, along with which streets would be our best bets. Since we would also be asking business and homeowners to put a Cahill for Congress sign in their window or on their lawn, the kids decided that we should hit those streets that got a lot of traffic. After consulting a map of the precincts, which we had obtained from the County Voters' Registrar's office, we also targeted areas with a large proportion of registered voters.

Since the kids had decided that encouraging people to vote was even more important than asking them to vote for me, we grabbed a stack of voter-registration forms to hand out to anyone who hadn't already registered to vote. We also had in hand copies of our flyers that Sam's and Ashleigh's moms had offered to photocopy.

"Are we ready to roll?" I asked.

Not quite, as it turned out. "We don't know what to say," Michael said. "Do we just hand them these things, say 'thanks,' and walk away?"

"Oh, gosh, no. You want to introduce yourselves."

We went over what constituted good manners—including saying "Yes, sir" or "Yes, ma'am" and "Please" and "Thank you"—and the fact that if they were really good with those, people would love them because not many kids speak like that anymore.

"Oh, okay," they agreed. "Good hint."

Then we practiced our manners.

"Michael, when you go to someone's door how should you stand?" I asked.

"I don't know."

"Well, should you be looking down at your shoes and slouching?"

He giggled, along with the rest of the group. "No!"

"Okay, so what do you think we should do about our body language?"

Nicole piped up. "Well, it's polite to make eye contact and say 'Ma'am' or 'Sir.' "

"Very good. Do you all agree?"

They did, though it was clear that they were still nervous. So we practiced several times with me pretending to be someone behind the door they were knocking on. I played the part of several different kinds of people so they could prepare for different scenarios.

"Yeah, what do you want, kid?" I snapped, pretending to open a door grumpily.

"Good afternoon, ma'am," Nicole said before launching into the spiel about our run for Congress that by now had become routine. "We're out encouraging people to vote," she concluded. "We'd like to encourage you to learn about the candidates and vote your conscience. If you don't know who to vote for and would like to support our teacher, we'd appreciate it. May I give you our campaign materials?"

"Who cares?" I responded. "I'm not voting for any of these idiots anyway."

"Well, thank you for your time, ma'am. If you have any questions you can call our teacher. Her number is right here on our pamphlet."

They broke into giggles as I made a final face and tried to be mean. Then we set out.

We started with my own neighborhood, where most of the homes had been built in the 1920s and '30s. The cool brick bungalows now mostly housed working-class or elderly renters. With many of the residents away at work, we ended up speaking largely to retired people who reminded me of my grandparents. To them, Election Day was like a national holiday; they always voted!

When the kids turned on their best manners, these older folks ate it up, just as I had predicted. One man in his early eighties opened the screen door, walked out onto the big porch, and shook each child's hand.

"It's wonderful what you're doing," he said. "It gives me hope for the future to see kids caring so much about our country."

I just about burst with pride.

My students were on their absolute best behavior the day a reporter from National Public Radio, Brian Behouth, joined us to tape the exchanges. Having an NPR reporter following us with a giant boom to catch the kids' interactions as they walked the precincts prompted a slew of questions.

"What does NPR mean, Ms. Cahill?"

"What radio station is that?"

"What does national mean?"

I explained that the radio station broadcasts different programs across the country.

"Wow! We're going to be on national radio," the walkers—Nicole, Sam, Michael, and Ashleigh—crowed. "That is so cool." When the piece hit international public radio later that week, they couldn't believe it.

"People in New Zealand might hear us?" Sam asked. "No way!"

After speaking to a number of elderly residents, we approached businesses on Wells Avenue, the main drag in this lower-middle-class part of town, where Mexican dress shops and eateries, tattoo parlors, and old Irish bars predominate.

"Sure, I'll take one," most of the store owners agreed. Even the owners or managers of those businesses that turned us down, like McDonalds, did so kindly, simply saying that they weren't putting up any signs at all.

When we passed the bar owned by eighty-something-year-old Mr. O'Gorman, a smiling itty-bitty leprechaun of a man with a big red bulgy nose, silver hair, sparkling blue eyes, and a pronounced Irish brogue, the kids balked. I knew him through his wife, who had worked at the Catholic high school all eight of their kids had attended, where I had taught for a year when I was just starting out.

"We can't go in there," they announced.

"I'm not taking you to a bar, honey, don't worry!" I said with a laugh, imagining how that would sit with the right-wing conservatives, or the press, for that matter.

During our monthlong vacation, the most-involved students also attended campaign events and media interviews. Often the focus turned more to them than to me, especially when Nicole or Ashleigh took over the microphone and began asking me questions as if they were the reporter. The press always cracked up at the girls' seriousness and polish. Boys like Paul, Sam, and Jordan also contributed, even though they weren't always too secure about going on and on about politics. Though a couple of the kids, including our art superstar, remained too terrified to talk on air, they loved being on camera. Even the shyest students ran home after a TV interview to count how many times they showed up on-screen. Michael, wearing a silver gray suit and a red bow tie, his hair carefully spiked with gel, would offer that cute little smile of his and gloat to his friends.

"Oh my god, that was so cool! Did you see me?"

Over the course of the campaign, we had remained the darlings of the Reno local news. During the last few weeks, the Las Vegas press would also eat up the story of our run for Congress, even though I didn't have the kids with me there. So the kids became increasingly sophisticated about media appearances.

One afternoon we headed to the local television news station for an interview. An assistant came and got us at the building's security checkpoint and escorted us to a room that looked like it might have been used for coffee breaks in the sixties. The old, dated furniture smelled as if someone had just finished a cigarette. After a few minutes, the woman who would be interviewing me, a contentious broad you wouldn't want to mess with because she could slice you up with her words, came to collect us. Danita Cohen looked more petite and frail than she did on TV, and I was surprised by how much makeup she had on. I suppose the studio lights made that necessary, though I certainly hadn't prepared for that.

When the tape that would air the following day at 6 a.m. on "Daybreak" started to roll, Cohen and her co-anchor, Sam Shad, who reminded me a little of the comedian Gallagher without the humor, asked us about my reasons for running and our campaign strategy.

Not exactly the hard-hitting questions I was expecting, I realized with relief.

I answered and then looked at my cohorts on the blue-and-gray set. That was Ashleigh's cue to take over. After reeling off the basics about what we were trying to prove and what we'd done so far, she put in a plug for the campaign.

"If you'd like a campaign sign or if you'd like to donate to our campaign you can reach us at Sarah Winnemucca Elementary. The number is 775-746-5810."

When we finished the mini-interview, the local TV personalities offered to show my students around the news station. Of course the kids wanted to see everything.

"I think what you're doing is really, really neat. Yay for you for getting involved," Cohen told them as we toured. "I'm so impressed with the job you're doing and how well you present yourselves."

As the kids beamed, Nicole held out the campaign contribution can we always carried during our outings.

"You know, we're not supposed to be biased at all about politics or campaigns," the typically brash newscaster said. Then she slipped a twenty in the can.

"Wow, even the press is giving us money!" my campaign staff exulted on the way home.

My students' support buoyed me on those days when I felt that I couldn't go on. One day, as we passed by a Jim Gibbons billboard by my house, the five or six kids with me stood below it and turned around so the Cahill for Congress message on their backs countered my opponent's ad. Every morning when I pulled off my side street onto Wells Avenue and saw the ad, that mental image made me smile.

Countering the lack of more formalized support, however, proved more difficult. So when the NPR reporter asked me about what kind of aid I'd received from the Democratic Party, I told him the god's honest truth. None. There-after, during follow-up interviews for local stations in cities like Washington, D.C., and New York, the interviewers rou-tinely asked me, "So are the Democrats helping you at all?"

And I continued to tell the truth. "No [pause], they're not."

"Why do you think that is?" they asked.

It was hard to be diplomatic, though I tried. I couldn't very well say, "Well, I wasn't given permission to run" or "Be-cause I'm not part of their inner circle," even though I thought that. Instead, I simply said, "I don't know. I can't speak for them or their motives. Maybe you should ask them."

Eventually, I confronted the county party myself. "Are you sabotaging me?" I asked Shane Piccinini, the head of the Washoe County Democrats, one night. "Why don't you have any of my signs or buttons at this event or at any other events, for that matter? Why do you have nothing from my campaign when every other Democratic candidate is repre-sented here?"

"Oh, we must have forgotten them at the office. Sorry."

"Really! If you forgot Al Gore's campaign material, I bet you'd go back and get it."

I knew I sounded paranoid, but I no longer cared. This had happened repeatedly. Originally miffed that I hadn't gone through channels, they were even more miffed that I wasn't just sucking it up and staying quiet like a good little girl. But honestly, when you have a candidate who wins the primary, I don't care if you don't spend any money on her— but at least let her play the game for the voters' sake. Be-cause if you're not helping your candidate, then you're hurting her. And who are you helping then? The opponent. Jim Gibbons's record on every issue the Democrats cared about was atrocious across the board. How could they not at least root for someone trying to go against him?

How many other candidates have they done this to? I wondered. *How much other new blood has been discouraged from participating in my party?*

I suddenly realized why the Republicans have gained such a foothold. They do a great job with what amounts to farm teams. They bring a lot of their right-wing nut jobs up through the ranks in local government: city, county, school boards, and the like. By grooming their people in the trenches, they wind up controlling everything from school boards (which allows them to determine what kinds of textbooks go into schools and to turn "evolution" into a bad word) to state politics (which allows them to reject gay-marriage initiatives). All because in contrast to the Democrats, they have done a good job of recruiting, training, and nurturing strong new candidates.

It made me sick.

21

Vegas Showdown

★ ★ ★ ★ ★ ★ ★ ★ ★ ★ ★ ★ ★ ★ ★ ★ ★ ★

"I would like to speak with Tierney Cahill, please," the woman on the phone announced in a voice that harbored no trace of uncertainty.

I had settled down to enjoy an afternoon in the sun and the now-rare privilege of seeing my son Kelton play ball. As I watched him trot out to take his first-base position in the run-down ball field, I thought yet again about how odd it was that his league, which pulled from the wealthiest as well as the poorest neighborhoods, played in one of the city's most run-down ballparks. The baseball diamond was located in a seedy part of town that I wouldn't want to walk in alone at night, near one of the city's huge casinos. Like so much of Reno, a hodgepodge of businesses had simply grown up around this weird pocket.

Though it certainly showed its age, the playing field itself wasn't too bad. The city maintained the outfield, and the league took care of the infield. The players' dads—usually those with more disposable money and time—did a pretty good job of keeping that field green. They also dominated the game when it came to coaching, even though a lot of our stars were the poorer ethnic kids.

The fifth inning had just concluded when my cell phone rang.

"This is Tierney," I said in response to the caller's declaration. Sensing some serious attitude, I already wished I hadn't picked up.

"Really? This is Tierney Cahill?"

"Yes, ma'am, how can I help you?"

"Well, I sure would like to know who the hell you are and what your whole deal is because I don't know anything about your campaign," said the woman, who eventually identified herself as Linda, a volunteer in Nevada's Democratic Coordinated Campaign/Get Out the Vote office in Las Vegas. Since Nevada was a swing state that could go either way in the presidential election, the Democratic National Committee (DNC) had funneled a ton of money into our state, set up the Coordinated Campaign office, and sent over a huge delegation of Washington, D.C., people to work for the Gore-Lieberman ticket. The other Democratic candidates on the slate were supposed to ride those get-out-the-vote coattails.

"I never heard of you," the caller continued. "I got no literature on you. And I have been calling on your behalf for days, and I'm so tired of people saying, 'Who is that?' and having to answer, 'I don't know who that is—I've never heard of her.' How am I supposed to get people to back you if I don't know who you are? How come I don't have a script for you? I need to know what to tell these people. Why don't you have your materials down here? We need signs, we need handouts, buttons, T-shirts. How come you're not taking care of business?"

Oh my god, this person is rude, I thought to myself as her tirade unfolded. I finally interrupted. "You know what, lady?

First of all, I'm a teacher, okay? I started this whole thing as a project."

Realizing that my voice had started to rise, I made my way out of the old wooden stands and started for my car as my anger spilled out.

"I never meant to win the damn primary, but I did! And now I'm your candidate, and I'm sorry, but I don't have a ton of money. I don't have bazillions of resources here. It's not like the Democratic Party is helping me at all. I appreciate you calling people on my behalf. What can I tell you about myself?"

"They're not helping you at all?" she asked, instead of answering my question.

"No! They're not giving me any money. And aside from having you make calls, which is news to me, they've done nothing to help me. Absolutely nothing."

"Really? Tell me more about your family."

"Well, I'm a single mom and I have three school-aged children," I said, launching into why I felt I was a good Democrat. "My children are brown, for god's sake, and I'm a union member."

"Wait a minute—so you're a single mom with three half-black kids?"

"Yes!"

In a second, she decided that the party's lack of support was racially motivated.

"They're prejudiced!" she exclaimed. "They're being prejudiced against you!"

"I don't know if that's true, and I doubt that's what this is all about! Maybe financially prejudiced. But I'm certainly not in with the party insiders."

"We need to get you down here. You gotta get down here

right away because there are all these events that are going to be taking place."

I reminded her about my campaign's limited funds.

"Oh, you'll just stay with me. You'll be fine. We'll pick you up at the airport. We'll have a driver for you and everything. We'll set up this itinerary and get you everywhere you need to go."

"Stay with you?" I asked, my anger quickly shifting to astonishment. "Are you sure?"

"Oh absolutely, absolutely."

We talked almost every day from then on.

"You're my new project," she announced. "I've been giving all my time to the Coordinated Campaign. I'll still go down there and call and everything, but we gotta get you going. Do you have a website?"

She called me back as soon as she had looked at it. "That's horrible! You need to have patriotic music for starters."

While that seemed over the top, her candor was refreshing. In an arena where duplicity and doublespeak are an art form, Linda said exactly what she thought. And after months of trying to be optimistic in the face of such odds, it was wonderful to find someone so impassioned and enthusiastic.

I landed at the Las Vegas airport on October 17, just three weeks before the election, feeling nervous. I didn't know who would be picking me up. Besides, although I did like her, Linda sounded a little crazy on the phone.

Lawana, the young woman who would be my attaché for the next three days, met me holding a handwritten sign with my name. She was tall, thin, gorgeous, and downright adorable in her dress slacks and blouse, with her supershort black hair cut like Halle Berry's. I quickly discovered that she could easily have functioned as a Congressional aide. As soon as we reached her Honda Civic, the twenty-two-year-old handed me a typed itinerary.

"I've been told to take you back to the house and let you freshen up and have something to eat," she said. "Then you have appointments today, okay?"

That was more than okay. What a relief to have someone else calling the shots for a change!

Linda's house, located in North Las Vegas, brought to mind old military housing: cheaply built with absolutely no architectural interest. The Section-Eight neighborhood, with dirt instead of lawns and broken-down cars in the front yards, reminded me of the year my ex and I had spent in Compton. I was far more unnerved about staying with someone I had never met than about staying in a poor African-American neighborhood.

Linda, a very large woman with very short hair, glasses, and a wandering eye, greeted me in a muumuu. By now I knew that despite a disability, she supported her family, made up of Linda's three children, ages ten to eighteen, her niece Lawana, and Lawana's baby, who Linda frequently cared for, as well as a homeless Caucasian gay man dying of AIDS, who would show up every now and then to take a shower.

"Don't be afraid if you see Ted," she told me. "He looks scary and he probably smells, but he's a good person and he needs a place to have some dignity and to clean himself, so our home is available to him. He panhandles out on the strip all day long and most times he'll sleep out there. But sometimes if he doesn't get enough money to get anything to eat or if he needs to come and clean himself, you'll find him here."

I didn't expect that kind of a giving, powerhouse woman to feel insecure about my presence, but she clearly did. I tried to dispel her nervousness right away by being as down-to-earth as possible. It wasn't like Al Gore was staying at her place. I wasn't some big dignitary, I was a schoolteacher. In the living room, actually a converted garage, I talked to her about her three kids and finally managed to put her at ease.

Linda and Lawana showed me to a neat room with a twin bed. As with the rest of the three-bedroom house, it looked like they had scrubbed it from top to bottom. When I found out that I would be dispossessing Linda's daughter, I felt terribly guilty, but Linda assured me that her daughter would just sleep with her.

Since we had a couple of hours before my first meeting, Linda and Lawana offered me breakfast—a bagel with cream cheese, granola, yogurt, and orange juice—and then watched me eat.

"Won't you join me?" I asked, uncomfortable to be the object of such scrutiny.

"Oh, no. We don't eat that," Linda answered. "That's white-folk food."

I laughed so hard I almost spewed my orange juice through my nose. "Well, what will you have for breakfast?"

When she replied that she would make a pot of grits once I was off, I told her to please serve me whatever her family normally ate. I felt guilty that they had spent their limited resources to try to make me feel comfortable.

When I finished my meal, Linda got on the phone and started to work her magic.

"On this leg of her campaign, Tierney Cahill will be showing up at [such-and-such a place] and then squeezing you into her itinerary because she is quite busy this week," I overheard her tell someone. I cracked up. She made me sound like I was the president or something.

At noon, I met with one of the area's most powerful black

preachers. Lawana and I drove to his home with the goal of gaining his acceptance. The reverend—a frail, elderly gentleman in a wheelchair whose blessing apparently had the clout to garner the support of the entire black community—talked to me about poverty and the challenges young blacks face when it comes to finding jobs and dealing with drugs. He was concerned about their education levels, as well as how many black males were in prison.

When I told him that my ex-husband was black and my children were biracial, that I had taught in Compton, California, and that I certainly shared his concerns for the community, he raised his eyebrows. I clearly wasn't just some blonde showing up and giving him a line. I had worked and lived in those communities and had at least some understanding of what was going on, although admittedly I will never truly know what it's like to be black and face their challenges.

From there, Lawana and I toured the Democratic Coordinated Campaign Headquarters with a field organizer named Dan, a sharply dressed, friendly African American who took charge of volunteers.

"Hi! Really good to meet you!" he exclaimed and I actually believed him. He seemed genuine, without any of the self-important airs so many others put on.

I wanted to personally thank the people who had been making calls on my behalf, so he took me around the entire building and introduced me to the volunteers. Most of these just-out-of-college kids had never even seen a picture of me. Linda alone was responsible for the fact that they actually knew who I was. Since there was no literature about my candidacy, she had opened her mouth and squawked about me, to make sure they knew my story and my politics. That way when they called individuals asking whether the party could count on their vote for presidential candidate Al Gore, Senate candidate Ed Bernstein, and House of Representatives candidate Tierney Cahill, they would be prepared to answer the inevitable "Who the hell is that?" questions.

Usually the Democratic Party contacts the various campaigns to make sure information is supplied. But until Linda called on her own accord, I didn't even know that it worked that way. Though I found it interesting that the party had given substantial amounts of money to other candidates and not a penny to me, I tried hard not to buy into the conspiracy theory that Linda had begun to expound. On the other hand, no one had even bothered to request my bio, which had my positions on every issue and which could also have just been printed off my website.

I forced myself to turn my thoughts back to the present as Dan explained how the Coordinated Campaign worked. "We're focusing on this precinct, for example, because it's a high Democratic one," he said, pointing to a map marked with numbers. "Teams will go out and pick up elderly voters who can't drive, and take them to the polls."

All the people in this huge building reinforced the vastness of the operation and the organization. Like busy little ants, they marched in and out to complete their targeted assignments.

"Okay, I need more signs. I've got to go put them out!" someone said.

"Wait, where's the map?" another countered. "Where do we need signs?"

Wow, I wish I had known about this earlier, I thought with more than a little resentment. I would have had signs and buttons here, along with the campaign literature Linda had requested. I would have even come down earlier and met those who would be contacting voters on my behalf. The more I thought about what I had missed out on, the more disappointed and frustrated I became. Upon my return home, I drafted a scathing e-mail to the head of the national Democratic Party, blasting him for not supporting all the party candidates.

"What's so disappointing to me is that I bought into the whole ideology behind the Democratic Party so deeply in my spirit that I named my daughter after Bobby Kennedy," I wrote. "I believed that carrying the legacy of the Kennedys and the Democratic Party would inspire her to do great things in her life."

Back at Linda's house, *Las Vegas Sun* reporter Susan Snyder showed up for the interview that my new campaign asset, Lawana, had lined up.

"You're staying here?" she asked, her eyes wide. "Okay."

She was clearly in absolute shock that a Congressional candidate was residing in that neighborhood for three days. The article "Teacher Teaches Us a Lesson" was the first to actually focus on me as a candidate rather than a cuteness factor.

The interview with Snyder ran long, which meant that I missed going to McCarran Airport to meet with vice presidential candidate Joe Lieberman's wife. Just the fact that Linda had orchestrated that opportunity blew me away.

"Are you kidding?" I said.

"Well, I have ways to get you in."

"Would I really have met with her?" I asked.

"No, but we would have loved those pictures of you right there with her," she said, adding that since Hadassah Lieberman would attend the final presidential debate at the union hall in Henderson that same evening, we could potentially make it happen then.

The party's goal that night was to maximize the grassroots

campaign effort by charging up those who attended. They would be the foot soldiers who would walk precincts and hit the phones for one last push. All of the bigwigs were there—Senator Harry Reid, Senator Dick Bryan, State Attorney General Frankie Sue Del Papa and the local Las Vegas people, including Dario Herrera, a Las Vegas candidate who was a darling of the party. A huge screen hung in the massive hall, where approximately 750 people, many wearing campaign T-shirts and carrying signs, gathered to cheer their candidates.

Linda's promotional plans didn't materialize. Though I was one of the candidates on that slate, I sat in the crowd with the rest of the people since no one had invited me onstage alongside the vice presidential candidate's wife. I'm sure it was an "oversight," but I'm equally sure that my opponent wouldn't have been in the stands. Lawana was more annoyed than I.

"Why weren't you on that stage? What's that all about?" she whispered heatedly in my ear.

"Well, Lawana, it's been like this the whole time. It's not a very friendly relationship. But this isn't our battle to fight right now. We just have to do the best we can."

On the other hand, not being on the stage gave me a chance to visit with real people who had real problems. A divorced father talked to me about how biased the courts are against men when it comes to child custody. Though he was already paying his ex-wife 27 percent of his pretax income, she refused to adhere to their agreed-upon child visitation schedule. When she did allow a visit, she'd send the kids with no clothes so that he'd be forced to buy them new ones. "The courts are so terribly slanted toward women. I don't understand it," he said. "She's got a drug problem."

I felt terrible for him.

"Please help me," he pleaded. "Please, please get elected so that you can help change this."

Following the public event, a private dinner for high-end donors to the Gore-Lieberman campaign was held at Andreotti's, an expensive restaurant in the Harrah's casino that I would never have been able to afford in a million years. Somehow I was allowed in past the Secret Service, who were mounting guard over the entrance like the British guards outside Buckingham Palace. Though I saw Senate candidate Ed Bernstein working the millionaires in the room whose checks for the Gore-Lieberman campaign were already being collected on silver platters, I couldn't bring myself to ask for contributions. I felt too uncomfortable not knowing any of these people. My self-consciousness about my lack of jewels and my scuffed pumps made trying to build a rapport with them even more challenging.

Though I hadn't eaten all day and wanted nothing more than to have a real meal, I didn't dare help myself to the hors d'oeuvres or handmade chocolates being passed out by waiters dressed in tuxedos and white gloves. I didn't want to get food stuck in my teeth or spill something down my front. It just wouldn't have been very ladylike. Leery of being called a lush, I stayed away from the champagne as well. So at 10 p.m. when the head of the Coordinated Campaign—a fast-talking, manipulative East Coast guy who I didn't much care for—invited me to a late dinner saying that he had a number of guests who wanted to meet me, I agreed with a sense of relief that I might actually get something to eat.

He took us to one of the cheapest, nastiest buffets in town. I have a thing about buffets. I'm probably just weird, but having all that food sit there under lights as people cough and sneeze on it just seems gross. Disgusted by the buffet offering but starving, I grabbed a plate and then sat with the group, comprised of Lawana; the East Coast Mr. Slick, as I'd dubbed him; the volunteer coordinator, Dan; two other guys from the Coordinated Campaign; and one of Senator Reid's top aides.

Oh my god, Harry Reid sent someone to sit in on this, I thought. Since the Senator's son, Rory, ran the party for the state of Nevada, it made sense that he would want eyes and ears at a meeting that was clearly not going to be a simple meet and greet.

"So, Tierney, tell me about your family," Mr. Slick asked as we started to eat.

His question, totally unexpected, instantly set my brain racing.

What is this really about? Does he really care about my family or is he trying to gauge what kind of social class I come from?

"What do you mean, my family?" I asked. "Do you mean my parents?"

"Well, yeah, why don't you tell me about your parents and your grandparents?"

"My grandpa worked for a trucking company. My grandmother worked for the highway patrol as a secretary. Then they opened their own private insurance company with Farmers Insurance. My mother was union in the early part of her career when she worked for the public transit bus company in Sacramento; now she works for a telecom giant in upper management, where she's a high-level trainer without union protection and benefits. My father has passed away; he was an engineer who also belonged to the union at one time. My stepfather runs the public transit repair shop. He oversees the building of natural gas and electric-powered transit these days."

"Okay, yeah, so pretty middle class," Mr. Slick said.

"Uh-huh, pretty middle class. Yep, that would be us. I forgot: Irish-Catholic middle class, to be specific," I said, pausing between each descriptor.

"And your own family?"

Okay, here we go, I thought, wishing I could actually eat a bite of the food on my plate. I was so hungry by then that it had actually started to look palatable. It was hard to imagine that this man didn't already know most of the information I proceeded to provide. I figured that putting me in the hot seat was the party's way of putting me in my place for squawking during radio interviews about how it hadn't helped me.

As the grilling moved on, it got more contentious and insulting.

"So do you have a master's degree?" Mr. Slick asked after I had outlined my educational background at his request.

"No. I probably have enough credits for two masters' degrees, but no, I've never focused on that."

"Hmm, interesting. So you don't have a law degree either?"

"No! I'm a teacher," I snapped.

Finally he got to the point of the meeting.

"So you basically have no experience, no connections, nothing, and you're upset because we haven't backed you?" he asked, clearly trying to intimidate me.

"Well, I'm terribly disappointed. This is the party I've grown up believing in. If you had a poster child for the quintessential Democrat the party should be representing, I'm it. And I don't think you guys have done a very good job of supporting me as your candidate."

He answered by outlining the party's position. "Let me be clear here. It's like there's been a terrible accident, okay?

We have all these people being wheeled into the emergency room, and as triage doctors, you've got to try to figure out who you can actually save and where you're going to put your resources. If you have someone who you know is going to pass away in a half hour, you make him comfortable and give him pain medication so it isn't too painful, but you sure don't put all your resources there. You're going to try and save the person who might be bleeding to death but is salvageable."

"Wow, what a gruesome analogy, but okay," I said.

"So to put this in other terms, Ed Bernstein is salvageable. He's ten points behind in the polls, but that can be remedied. There's potential to save him, so we're putting a lot of money, time, and effort behind him. Al Gore—absolutely. This is a neck-to-neck, nose-to-nose race, and we're putting tons of money behind Gore. This is a swing state, and we need to make sure that we take this state for the presidential election. Of course, we want to take *all* the federal races and then if we can get the state legislatures and local officials, great. But the hierarchy would certainly go from federal offices down."

Hello, I'm running for federal office, I thought to myself.

"Then there's you," he concluded. "Didn't you do this as a class project? Isn't that what this is? You're not really running, are you?"

Could have fooled me, I thought.

"Yeah, you're somewhat correct," I replied. "It started out like that, with a goal simply to get on the ballot and prove that anybody could run. But—oops!—I won the primary, so I wasn't just a kids' candidate anymore. At that point, I took on a larger responsibility and obligation to the voters of Nevada to be the best candidate I could be."

"Well, I think that's very admirable. You've done an amazing thing and provided quite a stunning civics lesson for your kids," he said. "But you're never going to win. There's no chance. When we polled on you, most people have no idea who you even are."

Boy, yeah, and you guys haven't helped with that at all, I thought.

"We're polling right now. You're going to get just 5 percent of the vote—10 percent if you're lucky. So you're the one in the emergency room who's going to die. There's no doubt, and we would just like to make you comfortable."

"Comfortable? Really? And what does that mean?"

"Well, basically, we would appreciate it if you would stop saying that we haven't done anything for you and that we haven't helped you at all."

Clearly this was about me making *them* more comfortable.

"But it's true," I said. "I don't bring it up, but when I'm asked, I'm not going to lie. I think what you all have done is terribly wrong."

"Well, you may think that, but while we haven't given you any money, there are volunteers who call every day for you."

"They call for the whole slate, not just for me," I countered. "And how weird would it be if they didn't include a Congressional candidate? So I don't think I need to thank you too much for that one."

I glanced at Lawana's face. Her expression said, *Oh holy hell, here we are engaged in a war.* Nobody at the table interjected a word. They just stared, their heads moving back and forth as if watching a tennis match as Mr. Slick and I kept going at it.

"Nonetheless, those calls represent time and money, and we're doing that for you. When we walk, we make sure that all candidates are represented."

"How is that possible when you have none of my materials—none?" I demanded. "So you're not putting up signs for me, you're not handing out campaign material door-to-door for me. The only people who have done that are the AFL-CIO, and thank god for them because they've done that statewide."

"You should see that as Democratic support because they're so widely Democratic," Mr. Slick rejoined.

"Well, I don't!"

He clearly wasn't going to budge. He just wanted me to shut up, stop being a pain, and die quietly. And I wasn't going to do that.

I turned to Senator Reid's aide.

"I don't know who's paying for dinner here, but thank you very much. While I appreciate your willingness to take us out to dinner, this meeting is over. Bottom line, I'm not going to be quiet—I'm going to continue to work hard, I'm going to continue to campaign hard, and do everything I can up until the last minute because I owe that to a whole lot of people, starting with my class. But I also have a moral obligation to the voters of Nevada, who deserve to have a candidate willing to fight for them till the end. You're saying that I'm the joke, that I'm not very serious, but how much did you all try to help bring me into the fold? Ultimately you're the ones who cheated the voters, not me. It's your fault they didn't have a better candidate. I've done the best I can do—I don't know if you can say that."

Now that I'd started, I couldn't stop. Months of anger and frustration continued to spew out of me.

"By writing me off, you've screwed the people of Nevada out of a real choice. Assuming I was a lost cause because I didn't have a million dollars to run a campaign is the exact reason so many Americans have become so cynical about our political system. I've probably been one of the best candidates in the state representing our party! So you can shove your 'you should be grateful' attitude, because you've got it backward. *You* should be grateful—I'm doing a damn good job of making this party look good."

If they hadn't known it before, they definitely knew now that I was an Irishwoman!

The next day Dan told me that upon their return to the campaign office, Mr. Slick concluded that I was "a raging bitch," ridiculously principled and idealistic on my high horse.

"Yeah," agreed one of the others who had sat quietly through the showdown. "But she was right."

22

The Final Push

★ ★ ★ ★ ★ ★ ★ ★ ★ ★ ★ ★ ★ ★ ★ ★ ★ ★ ★

"Listen, we clearly got off on the wrong foot," Nevada Democratic Party's executive director, Janice Brown, said over the phone as I packed my bags to return to Reno. "You've done a very good job and surprised a lot of people with your abilities and the way you've been able to present yourself. You're a good candidate."

She proceeded to add that the party owed me an apology for not helping with advice, manpower, or funding.

"There isn't as much money to give as people think, and we do have to focus our resources, so that wasn't directed toward you personally," she said. "It's just the way things are. Still, I'm sorry. I hope you'll consider running again, and if you do we would make sure you had a very good campaign manager and solid support because we think you have a lot of potential. If there's anything you need, we'd like to help you between now and the end of the election. So just let us know."

I returned home with the satisfaction of knowing that I had finally been heard—not just by the voters, but by my own party. Of course, since I had forgone sleep almost completely during the Vegas marathon of media events, interviews, meetings with prominent opinion makers, and public appearances, I was also sick, and my voice was so hoarse that it barely worked.

In a rare act of kindness, my usually self-centered boyfriend, Derrick, surprised me by whisking me to the beach in Los Angeles for a few days of rest. The evening we arrived, he had made arrangements to meet some old friends for dinner.

"Just go," I told him.

Although I knew that my relationship with Derrick had deep-seated problems, it felt nice to have someone look after me, order me hot tea, keep the curtains drawn so I could sleep, and take messages for me so I wouldn't be awakened by calls. Derrick could be downright charming and even nurturing when he wasn't drinking or feeling insecure.

I lay down in the hotel bed and fell into the deep sleep I so desperately needed, then spent the next day hanging out in a cozy restaurant by the beach eating chips and salsa and drinking margaritas. I didn't want to talk to or see anybody—my poor voice was dying and I was a mess. That night, the owner of a restaurant plastered with photos of Richard Nixon brought me a cup of tea loaded with honey.

"Protect your voice," he told me, even though he had been apprised of my Democratic status. "That's one of your most valuable assets."

By the following day, anxious about the campaign, I was a maniac.

"I've got to get back. I've got to get back," I told Derrick.

The last week of the campaign launched me back into hyperdrive. One morning I went to the union hall in Sparks at 4 a.m. to thank the trade guys gathered there for hitting the streets with door hangers listing the candidates they had endorsed. I was just one of four people on that slate, but expressing my gratitude to them was as polite as it was politically expedient. I knew that after two hours of walking that morning, they would be reporting for ten-hour shifts. That same night, after a day in the classroom, I returned to the union hall for a presidential rally also attended by Senators Harry Reid and Dick Bryan, State Legislator candidate Dario Herrera, and State Attorney General Frankie Sue Del Papa.

"Do you want to say a few words?" Senator Bryan asked.

I got up and spoke about why I felt vouchers were wrong for our country. "Even though I loved Bishop Manogue Catholic High School, where I used to teach social studies and where wonderful things are going on, I don't think it's appropriate for tax dollars to be funding private schools, because they have an entrance exam, they aren't required to provide special education, and they can kick children out at will if they're not performing or if they get in trouble. Public schools can't do that."

Looking at the audience, I spotted Casey Sullivan, one of my past students from that school, now in his twenties and nicely dressed in a suit.

"When you taught me I always thought you were a whack job," he told me after the speeches were over. "You talked so much about justice, tolerance, and ending discrimination. You always wanted us to go out and change the world. I thought you were a bit goofy and dramatic. But as I got older, I kept thinking back on what you tried to teach me and realized how right you were. I want you to know, Ms. Cahill, that I'm a Democrat today because of you. And I work for Senator Bryan."

"You're kidding!" I exclaimed stunned.

He looked at my ten-year-old son, Kelton, whom I had brought along to the event. "Your mother was very influential and valuable in my life. You're a lucky kid to have her as your mom."

Of course my kid answered, "Huh? Her?"

Casey asked me to attend the senator's retirement dinner that same evening, but as I typically hadn't been invited, I didn't think that would be appropriate.

"Oh, please come," he urged. "You can be my guest."

"No, hon, I don't want to show up at a private party like that."

"No, really," he insisted. "Democrats from all levels, from local to state, will be there."

I declined. Not only did I feel uncomfortable about crashing the party that would clearly be filled with all the higher-ups of the Democratic Party, I was scheduled to speak at another event in Gardnerville that evening, a good hour-and-a-half drive away. And at this late stage in the game, I certainly couldn't afford to alienate any prospective supporters.

The countdown was on. With the election just days away, the relentless campaign crunch began to creep into my work schedule. Channel 1 in Las Vegas wanted to air a debate between Gibbons and me. The debate had originally been scheduled for October, but the Gibbons people asked to have it moved to the beginning of November. Since I had returned to school by then and no longer had the flexibility to travel, the station agreed to have me do the debate by phone during my lunch hour.

As a peace offering, Rory Reid surprisingly volunteered to pick up any costs related to a satellite feed. Although the news stations had never mentioned the possibility of doing a satellite feed, I suppose that was big of him, since I'd been fairly brutal and definitely a squeaky wheel about the party's lack of support.

On the appointed day, the television station called my classroom.

"We're fifteen minutes away," the producer told me as I hung on the line. He came back on the line. "We're ten minutes away."

A minute to airtime, the Gibbons camp finally called in. When the producer got back on the phone with me, he was screaming mad.

"You aren't going to believe this! You aren't going to *fucking* believe this!"

"Okay, what?" I asked.

"They canceled. They *backed out*!"

Apparently, the representative's aide had asked, "Did you mean West Coast time or East Coast time? Oh, we thought you meant West Coast time. That's not going to work for the Congressman then."

"That's a load of crap," fumed the television producer, now faced with dead airtime.

"You know, I'm disappointed because I really would have liked the opportunity to go up against him," I said. "I think I would have done okay. And it bugs me because the voters aren't going to get to hear that, and they won't get more information on both of us. But you do realize that Gibbons's camp was probably waiting for me to back out, assuming that I wouldn't be able to pull this off."

When I didn't flinch in this game of political chicken, the Gibbons people clearly decided to pull the plug as creatively as they could. I couldn't blame them from a political perspective. I had everything to gain and Gibbons had everything to lose. I'm sure his political consultants pounded him not to go ahead with a debate that he had been cornered into accepting.

With a day to go before the election, Kristin Gore, Al's daughter, came to town to speak at the College of Education at the University of Nevada, Reno, and I actually got invited to attend. A first! I took half a personal day and invited my oldest son, Kelton, to come with me. The campaign had started with children, and I wanted a kid to be there. I couldn't get permission to bring my students, but I certainly had the power to pull my own child out of class.

"You're the journalist of the day," I told him. "You're going to have to go back to the class and report on this because no one else can come along." Then I gave him a camera and told him to take as many pictures as he wanted of whatever he found interesting.

Upon our arrival, we were ushered into a classroom where all the dignitaries were gathered to meet Kristin, a gracious Hollywood writer in her twenties, before she was steered to the auditorium, where hundreds of future teachers had gathered. When she was brought in, Ed Bernstein stepped forward to introduce himself.

"Oh, yes, yes, yes," she said. "My father knows who you are. You've been working really hard. We know you've run a good campaign."

I stayed back as others greeted her, but eventually she looked past the circle of people surrounding her to Kelton. Reading his Cahill for Congress T-shirt, she smiled at him and then at me.

"You're the teacher who decided to run for Congress," she said, walking away from the crowd. "I'm so impressed with your story. You're unbelievable. My dad has been following you and he thinks what you've done is so cool! You've done such an amazing job."

I'm not stupid. I'm sure her advisors had briefed her on the way to the event about who would be there. Nonetheless, her comments meant a lot to me. They also impressed my son, whose jaw threatened to hit his chest as it dropped. He recovered quickly and proceeded to snap as many photos as his finger and camera allowed.

"I have the honor to say that this is my son Kelton," I said. "He's a fifth grader and is here today to be the journalist."

"Then we have to have a picture together," Kristin replied. "Would you mind snapping a photo of me and this young reporter?"

I loved her for that. *Hurray for you!* I wanted to say. *You just made my kid's day. He's feeling very important right now.*

Fifteen minutes before the rally, the organizers told me they wanted me to speak. I had long ago overcome my fear of crowds and public speaking, no matter how impromptu. My speech about vouchers and how they could destroy public education was greeted with cheers. "Yay, Cahill!" they screamed from the gallery, which included some of the education professors I'd studied under. I'd hit a home run on my last time up to bat . . . and in front of my son, to boot.

23

Losing the Battle,
Winning the War

★ ★

Election Day. I felt a surge of adrenaline just as I always do when the future of the country is being decided. Once the polls open and people start voting, every moment that ticks by brings hope and a little fear, since decisions are being made that will impact everything from your household to whether the country goes to war. Knowing that my name was on ballots in seventeen counties across the state had me more keyed up than usual. Fourteen months of work had finally come to fruition.

Up at dawn, I read the paper, drank my coffee, and mentally reviewed the day's events before dressing and readying the kids for school. I taught that morning, then prepared for the substitute who would be filling in for me that afternoon. Before leaving, I took a few minutes to speak to my class. Though I had received a letter from the House of Representatives advising me that the official orientation program for newly elected members of Congress would be held in less than a week, I knew that we couldn't possibly win the election. But I didn't even think about that. I just felt so much gratitude toward my class. After reviewing all the work we had done and how well they had performed, I thanked them.

"You inspired me to be a role model and to live what I believe," I told them with tears in my eyes. "That has changed my life, who I am, and how I think about the world."

I had known all along that this campaign would provide an invaluable lesson. I just hadn't figured that I would be among its students. My previous class's dare had forced me out of a box I had unwittingly crawled into. In the space of five years, I had gone from having what I thought was a good marriage, a successful business, a nice home, and financial security to having everything except my children taken away from me. I had lost my husband, lost my home, lost my business, lost my father, lost my estate, lost almost every material possession. Our family van had even been repossessed. I had been left with one ever-present question: What happens to us if we don't make it?

I don't think anyone realizes that they're living in—and working out of—fear. So you don't realize how that fear limits your own creativity, innovation, and ability to change. Operating from that place doesn't allow you to grow because you look at worst-case scenarios instead of possibilities. You can't put money away because you need money for today. You can't plan for down the road because everything is about survival mode right now. And it's easy to get intimidated by people with wealth and a sense of superiority.

Running for office helped me trust that I was a lot stronger and more in charge of my destiny than I had realized. And I was no longer afraid. I wasn't afraid of senators. I wasn't afraid of the press. I wasn't afraid of Jim Gibbons. I felt like I could do anything I wanted to do. And I owed much of that to my students.

Over the last fourteen months, I had learned that unless I was dealing with poverty, cancer, or war, things would probably be okay. I had come pretty close to qualifying on that first count, but somehow I had managed to keep surviving and plodding along. Our family didn't have a lot of money, but I had very good, hardworking children with kind hearts. Plenty of well-to-do people don't have half that much. So maybe the struggles we had gone through weren't all bad.

Seeing their mother reach for her goals despite the odds also wound up inspiring my three children to work for their own victories. Seven years after my run for Congress, my oldest son, Kelton, conquered his shyness and won his high school's talent show during his junior and senior years by doing a funny dance routine with his good friend Paul Sutkowie. After his performance on the football field made him the first All State football player from Damonte Ranch High School, he was offered a couple of full-ride scholarships from schools in the South, but he is proud to be playing for the University of Nevada. My daughter, Kennedy, as quiet as she is, sits on the student council and competes in varsity volleyball, basketball, and track as a freshman—she's amazing. And my youngest, O'Keeffe, who excels at anything he puts his mind to, is completely full of piss and vinegar. As my grandpa said to my mom about my siblings and myself, "Don't knock that out of them, they need a little of that to make it in this mean world." None of the three operates from a place of fear. And though they may not end up in Ivy League schools, they'll do just fine and be good people and productive citizens.

That afternoon with my mother by my side, I made my way to the polls followed by the press—they always like to get the candidates on camera as they head in to vote. Inside the voting booth and finally alone, I looked at my name on the ballot and let the elation surge over me. The moment ended as quickly as it had begun. I still had to orchestrate the campaign's grand finale.

The Cahill for Congress election party that night was to be held at Joe Bob's Chicken Palace. It's not swanky like the casino ballroom where Republicans and Democrats were holding their celebrations, but it's my kind of place— televisions in every corner, a pool table, dartboards, a nice horseshoe-shaped bar, and plenty of pub tables where you can eat hot wings and drink beer. Located at the southern end of town in what used to be pasture and farmland, Joe Bob's was the kind of place where no parent would worry about not having the right clothes.

The two hundred invitations sent out on Halloween read:

Dear Families, Students, Friends, and Neighbors:

You are cordially invited to attend the celebration party of Tierney Cahill, Democratic candidate for the United States Congress District 2 on Election Night, November 7. Come and celebrate my journey through the Democratic process with all the people who have helped me make this possible. I have had the support of so many dear people. I want to share this moral victory with those who have been there for me. This is a family/community event. Bring the kids! Hors d'oeuvres will be served as we watch the voting returns come in. Please RSVP so we will know how many to feed.

Time: 6 to 9
Place: Joe Bob's Chicken Palace
Dress: Patriotically ☺ Red, White, & Blue

Ms. Tierney Cahill
Candidate for United States Congress, District 2

All the students involved in the campaign, along with their parents and my family, friends, and neighbors, would be there. I had spent the $700 left in our war chest on the party so the kids would have all the food and soda they wanted. They deserved it.

I was still decorating the restaurant with banners, streamers, campaign signs, and balloons when my mom returned with Kelton, Kennedy, and O'Keeffe in tow. Kennedy had obviously asked her dad to straighten her hair, a sure sign that this was a special occasion. All three wore their campaign T-shirts and buttons.

Grabbing me, my mother whispered, "Tierney, your kids have no idea that you're not going to win tonight."

On the way to the restaurant, she had told them they should be proud of me for what I had accomplished. Barely listening, my kids had routinely agreed.

"But you know she's not going to win tonight," she said. "You're ready for that, right?"

They weren't.

"What do you mean?" Kelton demanded.

"Honey, she can't win this, but what she has done is really remarkable."

Tears started shooting out of his eyes.

"Grandma, you're horrible. Take that back! How could you say that? My mommy is too going to win! You don't know how hard she's worked! This was so hard for her. You have no idea, Grammy!"

"Honey, I know your mommy has worked really hard," my mom countered, but Kelton was beside himself.

"There's no way she's losing tonight. She wouldn't have done all this if she wasn't going to win. She's going to Washington, D.C. Of course she's winning."

I had never thought to tell my children that I would lose.

I figured I had to work as hard as I could because I might never get a chance like this one again and because I wanted to know that I'd done my best. But I had never stopped to think how devastated they would be when I didn't win.

I understood how all the sacrifices I had made to run for office would make no sense to a child. Why would I have missed out on all that time with them if I had known I was going to lose? Why would I have put them through all the other hardships associated with this campaign? Kelton was asking the same questions that I had asked myself all along. I tried to explain it to him so that he understood.

By the time the guests started to file in at 5:30 p.m., my son had recovered. Soon it was Party Central, with every chair filled and every booth and table packed. As the kids played pool and shot darts, parents drank beer and watched the returns come in. The coverage of the cliff-hanger presidential election, along with all the other results, started on the East Coast since those polls had just closed, and then spread across to the West. Any time the newscaster recapped the results in the Nevada races, the kids screamed, cheered, and clapped so loudly that they drowned out the TVs.

News Channel 8, the local station, came to cover our celebration and never left, even though they usually attend a multitude of election events. Their entire coverage that night emanated from our party, which I thought was a riot. In the midst of hanging chads and the presidential election hanging in the balance, the news channel interviewed as many of my kids as they could get on camera.

Early on we grabbed 20 percent of the vote. Then our numbers climbed to 24, then 25 percent.

"We're gaining on them," yelled the kids. "We're catching them."

Around 7 p.m., ABC's Peter Jennings announced, "And Tierney Cahill, the teacher running for Congress, is getting 28 percent of the vote right now."

"He's saying your name!" the kids shouted, jumping out of their seats. Unable to contain themselves, those already standing bounced up and down with excitement.

I was ecstatic myself. "Twenty-eight percent—are you kidding?" I exclaimed to everyone and no one.

By 8 p.m., Angie Wagner with the AP, who had interviewed me in Vegas, phoned the bar.

"You know, we're calling the race," she said.

Though I was prepared, my heart sank just a bit.

"Okay," I answered.

"You know you did really, really well," she said.

"Yeah, I'm pretty happy."

"You're at 35 percent of the vote right now," she said.

I about died. I could barely believe it.

The party honchos were wrong, I gloated to myself. *They definitely underestimated a teacher and children on a mission.* I had soundly beaten the Coordinated Campaign's prediction. Four years ago the guy on whom they had placed their bets had garnered approximately one third of the vote. Though I had spent a fraction of what he had and received no support from my party, I had gotten almost the same results as that anointed favorite. That was huge! My class and I had proved that anyone could run for office. The process had won.

That victory would feel no less sweet when all the votes were counted and the final tally revealed that I had garnered 30 percent of the vote and spent just seven cents per vote (as opposed to my precedessor's seven dollars a vote) to do it.

Realizing that to bring this full circle I needed to concede, I climbed on top of a chair. My friend Stacey's husband, Todd, put his fingers in his mouth and whistled to get the place to quiet down. Once the bar turned down all the TVs, I launched into the hardest speech of my campaign.

"Listen, I need to have your attention. I just received a call from the Associated Press and enough votes have been turned in that they're calling the race."

"Yay, we won!" the kids began to yell.

Oh my god—have you not been watching the TV? I thought to myself. But I said, "They're calling the race and they're projecting Jim Gibbons as the winner."

Silence and deadpan looks greeted my announcement. "Are you kidding?" said most of the faces looking up at me. Then many of my students burst into tears. Even their Republican parents had begun wiping their eyes. I had to turn this around.

"Wait, no. Why are you crying? This is not something I want you to be sad about!" I exclaimed. "We didn't win, but we sure didn't lose. You've accomplished nothing short of a miracle. They're saying right now that we have 35 percent of the vote. Nobody thought we'd get as much as 10 percent.

"Think about why we started this campaign. We set out to prove that anybody could run for office and wound up doing much better than anybody ever thought we would. Are you kidding? With you running our campaign, we won the primary, got national coverage for our race, and did better than many professionals. Look at the votes we're getting. We definitely proved that the average person can do this. We ran our primary and general-election campaigns on just $7,000. Imagine what we could have done with $17,000 or $27,000.

"Don't ever forget what we've accomplished, because you all have the power to go out and do this yourselves in whatever venue you choose. Don't ever let anybody tell you, 'Oh, you're not good enough' or 'Your family isn't con-nected enough' or 'You don't have enough money' or 'You're the wrong color' or 'You're not the right religion.' Don't ever allow anybody else to limit you. You are capable of taking on anything you want as long as you're willing to work hard enough and fight hard enough for it.

"We didn't win, that's true," I concluded. "But we have an awful lot to be proud of."

Cheering and more tears—happy ones this time—erupted.

"There's one more thing that I have to do," I said. "It's proper to congratulate the winner. I'm going to need to call Jim Gibbons and thank him for running a polite, clean race."

"Ah, we don't want to talk to him," some of the kids grumbled.

"Well, we do, because that's what's proper, and we need to be gracious in all of this," I insisted. "We've been that all the way through; we're not going to change now."

My best friend, Stacey, had helped me round up a num-ber for Gibbons the day before, so I placed the call.

"You know, the AP phoned and they project you as the winner," I said as every person in Joe Bob's Chicken Palace listened in. "I want to congratulate you. I have an awful lot of young people looking at me right now, and I think it's important for you to know that they've been paying close at-tention to our race this whole time. I think we both pre-sented ourselves in a way that can make them and their families proud. I want to thank you for that and for being very generous and kind and for running a good race. Just please remember when you do go to Washington that there are a lot of people who also voted for us, so make sure you speak for them too."

At the end of the evening, after most of the guests had finally left, O'Keeffe came up to me.

"I'm so sorry you didn't win," my seven-year-old said bravely. I hugged him tight, knowing that he had cried at the news. Luckily, the allure of Joe Bob's fried chicken had quickly reclaimed his attention.

Before leaving, my principal approached. Throughout the entire campaign, her support had been tinged with the concern that a parent might complain about something. Though none ever did, she had understandably lived in fear of having to do damage control.

"Watching you evolve over the years from your first year of teaching until now has been just amazing, Tierney," she told me, misty-eyed. "You are a very, very good teacher. You truly, truly love the children you work with. You invest in them. You believe in them. You lift them up. You inspire them. It is such an honor to be your principal, and I could not be more proud of you today if you were my own daughter."

Overwhelmed, I thought about what a serendipitous journey this had been. I felt like Cinderella. All the battles I'd had to fight and all the struggles had been worth it. We had presented ourselves well and had gotten our message across. The laborious and consuming nature of the process had made that feat all the more valuable. And for a whole year, I had had my two sixth-grade classes hooked. Most of the time, you'll lose four to eight kids' attention during a class. And that's on a good day. Suddenly I had kids who didn't want to miss school or miss doing their homework assignments because they didn't want their parents to say they couldn't be involved anymore. I had special-education students making the honor role. It was a teacher's dream come true.

24

Ms. Cahill Goes
to Washington

★ ★

It was hard to believe that our year of campaigning was really over.

"If you want to stay home tomorrow, I totally understand," my principal told me. "You must be so tired."

There was no way I was going to take the day off. My students were still going to be processing what had happened. They deserved to be able to work through anything they were worried about, upset about, or excited about. I wanted to be with them to discuss whatever they wanted. Besides, we were a team. It wouldn't have been right for me not to be there.

"Shouldn't you wear your campaign T-shirt today?" my mom, who was still visiting, asked as I got ready for work that morning.

I had worn that T-shirt every day for a year. "Mom, I don't have to wear that stinkin' shirt ever again."

"I think you should wear it one more day, just one more day," she insisted.

"Aw, god, all right," I answered.

As I tried to tame my hair, a largely unsuccessful morning ritual, I realized just how exhausted I was. I would have done anything to sleep two more hours. Over the next three months, I would be so tired that I would wonder whether I had chronic fatigue syndrome and would joke that I had a political hangover.

Today, however, I had to wrap up a yearlong campaign where it had started—in my classroom.

As I entered the school's multipurpose room, which housed our cafeteria and drama stage, on my way to the office, it looked like a Cahill parade had been planned. My campaign signs had been hung up everywhere, along with blue-ribbon streamers, flags, balloons, and flowers.

"Good lord, what's going on?" I asked.

In the office, the secretary told me that I had dozens of calls to return. I had thought we were done. Apparently not.

"Well, I'll have to catch up with them later," I said. "I just want to get down to my room."

"Wait, wait, I need to see you for a minute," my principal said, emerging from her office. "We're going to be on a different lunch schedule."

My colleagues had clearly planned a celebratory event, and just as clearly didn't want to enlighten me any further. I didn't push. Later that morning, a batch of four-inch paper die-cut stars was delivered to my classroom with a handwritten note directing me to have the kids tape them to their pencils.

Just what exactly is up? I wondered. I didn't have much time for speculation. The classroom phone started ringing almost as soon as I walked through the door, with media requests from far-flung places. Newspapers outside the United States were interested in our story. In addition, local reporters, TV news journalists with their cameramen trailing closely behind, and radio people all wanted to interview me and the kids, and watch us in the classroom environment.

Even the Wizard called. "Hey, do you know where I am?" he asked.

I hope you're not on the way to my room, I thought.

"I'm down in Carson City on the main drag. I'm holding up a sign that says 'Recount for Cahill.'"

That cracked me up. In the midst of the Gore-Bush hanging chads debacle, the rest of the country was waiting to see who the next president of the United States would be. And he was still focused on me.

That day, the kids ate lunch at their desks. Finally, we were summoned to the multipurpose room. All of a sudden, a big car pulled up and out stepped Jim Gibbons and his wife.

"Are you kidding me?" I blurted out loud. I'd met my opponent at events, but our longest conversation had been the prior night when I had conceded.

Oh my god, I have to give him a present, I thought. I ran to my classroom in a panic to find something. I scanned all the shelves and bookcases looking for a possibility and wishing that I'd had some advance warning so I could have asked my mom to help me find an appropriate gift. Then I saw it—the perfect present. At science camp earlier that year, we had made feather-topped talking sticks using character beads adorned with words like "friendship," "integrity," "hard work," and "honesty" that we had earned during the week. Throughout the year whenever things got out of hand in the classroom, I would bring out my three-foot-long talking stick and hand it to whoever was due to speak. Since only the person holding it is allowed to talk, order was immediately restored. When the speaker was through, he or she handed it to the next person.

This is a good gift, because he's going to have to go to Washington and talk on behalf of all Nevadans, I thought. *And these character beads should help guide him.*

It was hokey, I know, but that's how elementary schoolteachers think. We're idealistic.

As my class and I headed into the multipurpose room where seven hundred students gathered, all waving their star-topped pencils, one of Gibbons's aides pulled me aside.

"I've got to ask who designed your sign," he said.

I looked over at my group of kids seated on the floor with the rest of the school's students, unable to suppress a giggle. "They did," I said.

"They made this in your classroom?"

"Well, they designed it and then we took it to a graphic artist."

"That's incredible," he said. "This whole time we've been wondering how you managed to get such a slick-looking logo."

"Well, maybe you need to hire some sixth graders next time," I quipped with a laugh before heading to the stage. I couldn't wait to tell the kids.

As my principal introduced us, I noticed my mom and stepdad, along with my brother, sitting on the sidelines with the teachers. Running through how this had all started, just in case some of the younger kids didn't know, I recapped the campaign and the election results. I thanked my class for all their hard work and for making me a better teacher and a better human being. I thanked all the teachers and everyone who had helped me. And at the prompting of my principal, I thanked my parents for being there. I guess you're never too old to have someone remind you not to be a little brat. Then I introduced the Congressman, pulling out the talking stick as I spoke. After explaining how it worked, I told him that I felt he had good character, which would help him do his big job in Washington and speak on behalf of all Nevadans.

"So my dear friend, Mr. Gibbons, I present you with this talking stick," I concluded.

The place went nuts. Children cheered right along with my principal and much of the staff. Seeming a tad over-whelmed, Gibbons accepted my offering and we hugged each other, showing all the students that you could be friends with an opponent and even downright affectionate.

"I'm sure glad that this race wasn't just run at this school because there's no way I would have won," Gibbons an-nounced as he looked out over the crowd and all those wav-ing stars. "I don't know that I would have gotten any votes at all."

When the renewed cheers subsided, he once again com-plimented us on our race. After explaining what Congress was like, he said, "I too have a present." Then he handed me a pen developed by NASA that could write upside down.

"NASA spent all this money on a pen that didn't need gravity to make the ink flow," one of my sarcastic but funny students said later. "Why didn't they just use a pencil?"

Of course, that was after he—and all the other kids—had gotten to touch the pen, which thrilled them.

Gibbons's visit, which ended with a tour of the school and a visit to our classroom, helped reinforce the notion that campaigns don't have to be icky. That pleased me. I was even more delighted by a report from Ashleigh, a student who had started the year preoccupied by social concerns, to the detriment, I fear, of her academics. A very pretty girl who had developed early, she had been mercilessly teased by some of the less developed girls, who were clearly jealous of her figure, and by some of the boys, who just didn't know how to deal with their own reactions to her. That poor little thing would come in crying from recess all the time.

"Could I please just sit in the hall and get myself together?" she would say, not wanting to talk about what had happened. It used to kill me because she typically wore revealing tops and supershort skirts that helped provoke the awful treatment she received.

Finally I pulled her aside. "There's so much more to you than this cheerleader persona you're adopting," I told her. "You're more valuable than that. You're so bright. I just hate for you to wrap your whole identity around your looks and what lip gloss you're wearing and what boys think of you. Who cares what they think of you?"

Kids appreciate being treated like a human being by an adult who has taken the time to get to know them. You see them soften those fronts they try to put on if they know you're speaking from your heart. And often they'll reciprocate.

Ashleigh gained a ton of confidence over the year as she participated in the campaign. Though she had been really zipped up as a reaction to the mean treatment she had received, she discovered her voice in the two different committees she threw herself into. It was awesome to see her become more vocal and opinionated, and express her ideas forcefully and convincingly to her fellow students, as well as to reporters and to the people she met at all the events she attended with me. By the end of the year, the girl who had seemed so distant when she arrived in my class had transformed from a struggling student to a class leader who was often interviewed by the press. She eventually decided to attend a math- and sciences-oriented middle school, where she ran for student body president—and won. She would go on to successfully run for treasurer in high school and then

secure a snowboarding and academic scholarship to Sierra
Nevada College.

The summer following the election, having been offered
a graduation trip anywhere in the world by her single
mother, Ashleigh opted for Washington, D.C.

"Are you sure you don't want to go on a cruise?" her
mother asked.

"No, I want to go to Washington and see all this stuff that
we talked about," she replied.

Once in D.C., Ashleigh decided that she wanted to check
out Gibbons's office. So she and her mother made an appointment to go by even though the Congressman was out
of the country. Once there, Gibbons's assistant offered to
take Ashleigh's photograph, an offer the little media hound
jumped at. As she headed to his chair to have her picture
taken, Ashleigh spotted what she'd been looking for all
along—the beaded talking stick behind his desk. A piece of
Cahill for Congress had made it to Washington after all.

Notes

★ ★ ★

CHAPTER 2

25 Shawn Boskie (1985), www.renohighalum.com

CHAPTER 5

57 $9.6 million for a Senate seat, "Students for Clean Elections:
A joint project of Common Cause and Democracy Matters,"
www.commoncause.org/site/pp.asp?c=dkLNK1MQIw
G&b=2822449

CHAPTER 9

89 "I abated the nuisance," www.foxnews.com/story/0,2933,
292166,00.html

CHAPTER 15

156 suicide for those over sixty-five, www.hhs.unr.edu/chhs/bhn.
html

Acknowledgments

* * *

I'd like to thank the following people, without whose tremendous support and assistance this book would have been impossible:

The children of the class of 2000 and 2001, for asking me to be who I said I was. I'm forever grateful for your vision of what this world should be and how our country should work. You've given me hope for the future.

My parents, who raised an ornery, spunky, fearless daughter, for teaching me never to doubt the capabilities within myself.

My grandparents, Jim and Mary Stewart, for sharing values such as, *We owe something back* and *Make your life emulate your values,* which I still believe in and admire.

My children, for believing in their idealistic mother and tolerating my experiment as well as the impact it had on our lives.

My husband, the most precious and dearest man I've ever known, for pushing me to share my experiences, for adoring me, and for creating an amazing life for us.

My sister Cortney Peters, for our friendship and her never-ending support.

My dear, dear friend and co-author, Linden Gross, without whom I could never had created this type of book. Linden, your words and insights helped me convey the true story that lay within my heart.

Ted Weinstein, my agent, for taking my call and believing in my story. Your support and guidance were tremendous.

Julia Cheiffetz, my editor, without whom this project would never have come to fruition. I'm eternally grateful for your wisdom, insight, and support.

Penny LaBranch, the model of what a true educator is, for believing in me despite my risk-taking ways.

Stacey and Todd Melcher, my angels. Without your silent blessings, I don't know what would've happened to the cherubs and myself.

My sixth-grade team, Todd Herman, Linda Lamour, and Karen Bowman, for the coffee on those rough mornings and all their moral support.

The city of Reno and the State of Nevada. I'm blessed every day that I wake up and enjoy the magical life that exists here.

All the organizations and the people I love who constitute my village: Stephanie Kveum, Bill Harrison, Tony Amantia, Bev and Tony LaMonica, Tim and Laura McCartin, Bob and Debbie Hellen, Dawn Gibbons, Denise Hausauer, Eric Feeney, Darvel Bell, Ron Seckler, Rod Hearn, Kristina Wulfing, KOLO News Channel 8, *Reno Gazette-Journal*, Debbie Smith, Diane Hart, Kendall Stagg, Lynn Warne, AFL-CIO, NEA, Elaine Lancaster, Danny Thompson, John Martini, John Cassani, Frank and Sidney Stewart, Mike and Judy Stewart, Sara Williams, Sally Greig, Tod Young, Bill Ames, Buffie Olack, Gary Firstenberg, Alicia Gordon, Trevor Engelson, Nick Osborne, Eric Elfman, Neil Schusterman, Marisa Yeres, Elain Goldsmith-Thomas, Random House, DreamWorks, CJ and Joey Skog, Cathy Linde,

Nancy O'Hair, Cynthia and Jim Richardson, Bruce and Kathy Nelson, Tavia Williams, Treva Williams, Paul Dugan, Steve Mulvenon, Lamont Hall, Brian Behouth, Eric Franke, NPR, PLAN, Las Vegas Linda, Dennis Hof, and Dr. Coretz Williams, Ph.D.

ABOUT THE AUTHORS

TIERNEY CAHILL currently teaches English to middle-school students and social studies to high-schoolers. She also tutors struggling students on her own time and coaches middle-school basketball and varsity softball. Formerly a Washoe County School District's Multicultural Representative, she has served as an elected local, state, and national teachers' union representive. In 2000, nominated by her students' parents, Cahill was awarded the Best in Education Award from the *Reno Gazette-Journal,* as well as the Women's Role Model Award from Nevada's attorney general.

LINDEN GROSS is a bestselling author and co-author. She ghost-wrote Julia "Butterfly" Hill's national bestseller *The Legacy of Luna* (HarperCollins, 2000) and has co-authored three other books. She is the sole author of *Surviving a Stalker: Everything You Need to Know to Keep Yourself Safe* (Marlowe & Company, 2000) and *To Have or to Harm* (Warner Books, 1994), the first book written about the stalking of ordinary people. Gross is also the founder of www.stalkingvictims.com and of the Stalking Survivors' Sanctuary and Solutions, a nonprofit organization.